The Iraqi Prisoner Abuse Scandal

The Iraqi Prisoner
Abuse Scandal

Titles in the Lucent Terrorism Library include:

America Under Attack: Primary Sources
America Under Attack: September 11, 2001
Civil Liberties and the War on Terrorism
The History of Terrorism
Terrorists and Terrorist Groups
The War Against Iraq

THE
LUCENT
ERRORISM
LIBRARY

The Iraqi Prisoner Abuse Scandal

Michael J. Martin

LUCENT BOOKS

An imprint of Thomson Gale, a part of The Thomson Corporation

THOMSON

™

GALE

Detroit • New York • San Francisco • San Diego • New Haven, Conn. • Waterville, Maine • London • Munich

On cover: *A hooded Iraqi detainee appears to be cuffed at both wrists and collapsed over a rail at Abu Ghraib prison.*

LIBRARY OF CONGRESS CATALOGING-IN-PUBLICATION DATA

Martin, Michael J., 1948–
  The Iraqi prisoner abuse scandal / by Michael J. Martin.
    p. cm. — (The Lucent terrorism library)
  Includes bibliographical references and index.
  ISBN 1-59018-769-5 (hardcover : alk. paper)
  1. Iraq War, 2003—Juvenile literature. 2. Iraq War, 2003—Prisoners and prisons, Americans—Juvenile literature. 3. Abu Ghraib Prison—Juvenile literature. I. Title. II. Series.
DS79.763.M37 2005
956.7044'3—dc22
                                                                    2004023824

Contents

Foreword

It was the bloodiest day in American history since the battle of Antietam during the Civil War—a day in which everything about the nation would change forever. People, when speaking of the country, would henceforth specify "before September 11" or "after September 11." It was as if, on that Tuesday morning, the borders had suddenly shifted to include Canada and Mexico, or as if the official language of the United States had changed. The difference between "before" and "after" was that pronounced.

That Tuesday morning, September 11, 2001, was the day that Americans began to learn firsthand about terrorism, as first one fuel-heavy commercial airliner, and then a second, hit New York's World Trade Towers—sending them thundering to the ground in a firestorm of smoke and ash. A third airliner was flown into a wall of the Pentagon in Washington, D.C., and a fourth was apparently wrestled away from terrorists before it could be steered into another building. By the time the explosions and collapses had stopped and the fires had been extinguished, more than three thousand Americans had died.

Film clips and photographs showed the horror of that day. Trade Center workers could be seen leaping to their deaths from seventy, eighty, ninety floors up rather than endure the 1,000-degree temperatures within the towers. New Yorkers who had thought they were going to work were caught on film desperately racing the other way to escape the wall of dust and debris that rolled down the streets of lower Manhattan. Photographs showed badly burned Pentagon secretaries and frustrated rescue workers. Later pictures would show huge fire engines buried under the rubble.

It was not the first time America had been the target of terrorists. The same World Trade Center had been targeted in 1993 by Islamic terrorists, but the results had been negligible. The worst of such acts on American soil came in 1995 at the hands of a homegrown terrorist whose hatred for the government led to the bombing of the federal building in Oklahoma City. The blast killed 168 people—19 of them children.

But the September 11 attacks were far different. It was terror on a frighteningly well-planned, larger scale, carried out by nineteen men from the Middle East whose hatred of the United States drove them to the most appalling suicide mission the world had ever witnessed. As one U.S. intelligence officer told a CNN reporter, "These guys turned airplanes into weapons of mass destruction, landmarks familiar to all of us into mass graves."

Some observers say that September 11 may always be remembered as the date that the people of the United States finally came face to face with terrorism. "You've been relatively sheltered from terrorism," says an Israeli terrorism expert. "You hear about it happening here in the Middle East, in Northern Ireland, places far away from you. Now Americans have joined the real world where this ugliness is almost a daily occurrence."

This "real world" presents a formidable challenge to the United States and other nations. It is a world in which there are no rules, where modern terrorism is war not waged on soldiers, but on innocent people—including children. Terrorism is meant to shatter people's hope, to create instability in their daily lives, to make them feel vulnerable and frightened. People who continue to feel unsafe will demand that their leaders make concessions—*do something*—so that terrorists will stop the attacks.

Many experts feel that terrorism against the United States is just beginning. "The tragedy is that other groups, having seen [the success of the September 11 attacks] will think: why not do something else?" says Richard Murphy, former ambassador to Syria and Saudi Arabia. "This is the beginning of their war. There is a mentality at work here that the West is not prepared to understand."

Because terrorism is abhorrent to the vast majority of the nations on the planet, President George W. Bush's declaration of war against terrorism was supported by many other world leaders. He reminded citizens that it would be a long war, and one not easily won. However, as many agree, there is no choice; if terrorism is allowed to continue unchecked the world will never be safe.

The volumes of the Lucent Terrorism Library help to explain the unexplainable events of September 11, 2001, as well as examine the history, personalities, and issues connected with the ensuing war on terror. Annotated bibliographies provide readers with ideas for further research. Fully documented primary and secondary source quotations enliven the text. Each book in this series provides students with a wealth of information as well as launching points for further study and discussion.

A Dark Day in America

During the first week of May 2004 horrific photographs of American soldiers abusing prisoners in Iraq's Abu Ghraib prison were released to the public. The photos caused shock and outrage—both inside the United States and around the world. Seeking an explanation, Congress called Donald Rumsfeld, the secretary of defense, to appear before the Senate Armed Services Committee. "Let me begin by stating the obvious," said Senator Jack Reed speaking to Rumsfeld at the witness table. "For the next 50 years, in the Islamic world and many other parts of the world, the image of the United States will be that of an American dragging a prostrate, naked Iraqi across the floor on a leash."[1]

Reed's opening statement, of course, was only a prediction—no one knows for sure how the scandal will affect the United States over time. But there was little doubt that what had gone on inside a notorious prison just west of Baghdad had, at least temporarily, seriously hurt America's cause in the war on terrorism. That was obvious a few weeks later in the pained faces of members of Congress as they emerged from a darkened room in which they had just spent three hours viewing eighteen hundred slides and several videos of the abuses at Abu Ghraib. During those three hours they studied images of soldiers sexually assaulting Iraqi prisoners. Other photos showed American soldiers terrifying naked prisoners with attack dogs or humiliating them in front of grinning female guards. Even more shocking photos showed soldiers grinning and laughing alongside dead Iraqis whose bodies had been mutilated. Perhaps worst of all, no one seemed to have a sense that what they were doing was wrong.

Was This America?

The awful images shocked members of Congress into uncharacteristic silence. There was very little talking on their walk back to the floor of the House of Representatives. They were far from alone in their dismay. "It is horrifying to contemplate that U.S. interrogators have tortured and killed foreign prisoners and that their superiors have ignored or covered up their crimes—and yet that is where the available facts point,"[2] noted the *Washington Post.* Andy Rooney, commentator for the television show *60 Minutes,* expressed the sinking feeling of those who feared they were witnessing a low point in the nation's history:

This shocking image of an American soldier dragging an Iraqi prisoner on a leash is part of a photo exhibition exposing the abuses that took place at Abu Ghraib prison.

Our darkest days up until now have been things like presidential assassinations, the stock market crash in 1929, Pearl Harbor, and [the terrorist attacks of September 11, 2001], of course. The day the world learned that American soldiers had tortured Iraqi prisoners belongs high on the list of the worst things that ever happened to our country. It's a black mark that will be in the history books in a hundred languages for as long as there are history books. I hate to think of it. . . . The image of one bad young woman with a naked man on a leash did more to damage America's reputation than all the good things we've done over the years ever helped our reputation.[3]

International response to the images, especially in the Middle East, underscored Rooney's point. In the weeks after the scandal broke, pictures of the abuses at Abu

---

An Ugly Environment

In an article for Rolling Stone *magazine, Osha Gray Davidson referred to military documents to describe the horrendous conditions at Abu Ghraib in the fall of 2003—both for the prisoners and those guarding them:*

"The secret files make clear that day-to-day living conditions were 'deplorable' for soldiers as well as prisoners. The facility was under constant attack from mortars and rocket-propelled grenades . . . there were more than two dozen explosions between July and September alone. Six detainees and two soldiers were killed, and seventy-one were injured. . . .

The prison was filled far beyond capacity. Some 7,000 prisoners were jammed into Abu Ghraib, a complex erected to hold no more than 4,000 detainees. Prisoners were held in canvas tents that became ovens in the summer heat and filled with rain in the cold winter. One report found that the compound 'is covered with mud and many prisoner tents are close to being under water.' . . .

In a series of increasingly desperate e-mails sent to his higher-ups, Maj. David DiNenna of the 320th MP Battalion reported that food delivered by private contractors was often inedible. 'At least three to four times a week, the food cannot be served because it has bugs,' DiNenna reported. . . . He [also] reported that 'for the past two days prisoners have been vomiting after they eat.'

Officers reported that their repeated pleas for adequate food and supplies went unheeded, even though prisoners were attacking soldiers. 'I don't know how they're not rioting every day,' [Capt. James Jones of the 229th MP Company] told Taguba. The worst riot occurred on November 24th. . . . Three detainees were killed and nine were wounded. Nine soldiers were also injured in the riot."

Ghraib appeared almost continuously on Arab television and on the front pages of newspapers. The reaction of seventeen-year-old Nour Dandash, a Lebanese student, was typical. Staring in disbelief at a photograph of naked and hooded Iraqi detainees piled in a heap between two laughing American soldiers, Dandash commented: "It's sick, horrible, disgusting. The Americans say they went into Iraq to stop these abuses. But now they're doing exactly the same thing as [former Iraqi dictator] Saddam Hussein."[4]

Most Middle East newspapers featured pictures of smiling Americans brutalizing prisoners at Abu Ghraib on their front pages. Headlines asked whether this was an example of the democracy and freedom that President Bush had claimed the removal of Saddam Hussein would bring to Iraq. The prison photographs were particularly painful for Iraqis, because under Saddam's brutal leadership Abu Ghraib had long been known as a place of torture and execution. When Saddam was driven from power in March 2003, there was hope that those days were finally over. A year later the images of Abu Ghraib fueled intense anger. Iraqis felt that their expectations of a better future had been dashed. Qasim Alsabti, an Iraqi artist, spoke for many of his countrymen when he said, "It's like an adviser from Saddam Hussein's regime has come back to Iraq and is now advising the Americans."[5]

Apologies and Outrage

On April 30, 2004, Bush expressed his own revulsion, emphasizing his deep disgust at the inhumane way prisoners at Abu Ghraib were treated. But his public regret did little to ease the outrage over the scandal. Whether Abu Ghraib will indeed permanently tarnish America's reputation remains to be seen. But there is little doubt that when it was exposed, the Abu Ghraib prisoner abuse scandal damaged America's worldwide image as a country that respects liberty, freedom, and human dignity. Investigators will be spending years trying to figure out exactly how it happened.

Chapter One

Iraq and the War on Terror

The war on terrorism and the way it was fought inside Iraq helped create a climate that led to the abuses seen later at Abu Ghraib and other prisons. Iraq became an early focus of the Bush administration's war on terror. After terrorists crashed jetliners into the World Trade Center and the Pentagon on September 11, 2001, the official policy of the Bush administration was to go after regimes that support terror. Iraq was considered to be one of those regimes because its dictatorial leader, Saddam Hussein, was thought to have weapons of mass destruction that he could pass on to terrorists. Although little evidence was found linking Saddam with the September 11 attacks, public statements by administration officials suggesting that he must be dealt with soon caused many Americans to see him as a major enemy in the war on terrorism.

The administration's concern with Iraq remained high even after it was learned that no Iraqis had been directly involved in the plot. It turned out that al Qaeda, a terrorist organization based in Afghanistan, had actually planned and carried out the attacks. In October 2001 the United States invaded Afghanistan in order to capture or kill the terrorists responsible for the September 11 attacks. By December they had routed the Taliban, the government that had refused to turn over al Qaeda members. Yet, as the fighting in Afghanistan subsided, Bush and other administration officials insisted that Saddam Hussein's regime represented a terrorist threat to America—a threat so dangerous that the president must do everything in his power to ensure that Saddam was disarmed immediately.

Target Iraq

In the months that followed, the Bush administration continued to emphasize the danger Iraq represented to the United States. During his State of the Union speech before Congress in January 2002, Bush made it clear that he considered Iraq a big part of the war on terror. "Iraq continues to flaunt its hostility toward America and to support terror," he said. "The Iraqi regime has plotted to develop anthrax and nerve gas, and nuclear weapons for over a decade."[6]

The president also named Iraq as one of three countries—Iran and North Korea were the other two—that he believed constituted an "axis of evil."[7] Because these nations sought weapons of mass destruction, said Bush, they represented a growing danger. In the spring of 2002 he announced a

new doctrine known as preemptive war. This new doctrine asserted that, in self-defense, the United States had the right to attack any country it felt might threaten it in the future. As Bush said, "We must take the battle to the enemy, disrupt his plans, and confront the worst threats before they emerge."[8]

By the fall of 2002 it seemed increasingly likely that Iraq would be the first country where Bush's preemptive war doctrine would be tried out. In October the president made headlines when he claimed Iraq had "a massive stockpile of biological weapons that has never been accounted for and is capable of killing millions."[9] Then, during his 2003 State of the Union address, he raised the stakes higher by implying that Iraq had been secretly attempting to buy uranium, the raw material for nuclear bombs. The following month Secretary of State Colin Powell spoke to the United Nations. His goal was to get the UN to back a U.S. invasion of Iraq. In support of his case Powell asserted that Iraq had revived its nuclear weapons program and had tons of chemical and biological weapons it would not hesitate to use. During a long and forceful presentation Powell used satellite photos and even held up a vial of a deadly poison called anthrax. Powell failed to get the UN to support a war against Iraq (much of the information he presented that day was later proven inaccurate), but the speech persuaded many Americans that an invasion of Iraq was a necessary part of the war on terror.

Therefore, on March 19, 2003, the United States invaded Iraq. The U.S. military was joined on the battlefield by roughly forty-seven thousand troops from a coalition of other nations. The military aspect of the operation went exceedingly well. The coalition quickly gained control of the country with relatively few casualties. Although the invasion force found no evidence of weapons of mass destruction, by the end of three weeks they had fought all the way to Baghdad, Iraq's capital. As coalition troops entered the city, Saddam Hussein went into hiding and his government collapsed.

House of Horrors

Perhaps no one was happier to see Saddam Hussein go than the inmates of a notorious prison called Abu Ghraib. Abu Ghraib's history went back to the early 1980s. It was where Saddam sent political prisoners accused of criticizing him or plotting against his rule. Thousands of Iraqis who entered Abu Ghraib were never seen alive again. Located about twenty miles northwest of Baghdad, the huge prison sat upon 280 acres of dusty land and was surrounded by palm tree groves. High walls topped with razor wire and overseen by twenty-four guard towers made escape unlikely. Since each cell measured twelve feet by twelve feet and held as many as forty prisoners, living conditions were miserable. The peak population was about fifteen thousand prisoners, but weekly executions always made room for more. In 1984 alone, four thousand prisoners were put to death.

Under Saddam Hussein, Abu Ghraib and other prisons like it were known as places of torture, degradation, and execution. "I visited Abu Ghraib [in March 2003] . . . ," recalls Bob Baer, a former CIA

In his 2002 State of the Union address, President Bush identified Iraq as a significant threat to national security.

Razor wire and guard towers along the perimeter of Abu Ghraib made escape from the deplorable conditions of the prison virtually impossible.

bureau chief. "There were bodies there that were eaten by dogs . . . electrodes coming out of the walls. It was an awful place."[10] When Saddam was ousted by the United States in the spring of 2003, many Iraqis assumed those days had finally ended. Yet not long after the arrival of coalition troops, torture and mistreatment would once again take place at Abu Ghraib. And within a year of coming under coalition control the prison would become more notorious for its brutality than it ever had been under Saddam.

Up and Running Again

Although Saddam had been deposed quickly, the end of major fighting had not brought much peace to Iraq. There simply were not enough coalition troops in the country to ensure law and order. Some Iraqis came to believe that the coalition was more interested in the nation's rich oil fields than in their own freedom and security. Others, especially those who had been loyal to Saddam, were skeptical of their future under a new U.S.-backed government. Yet others were frustrated with the slow pace of reconstruction. Sewage plants operated sporadically, if at all. Electricity was only available for portions of each day, and blackouts were common. There were few jobs, and food and other basic services were scarce.

There were also not enough policemen to prevent a huge upsurge in crime and violence. For all these reasons, some Iraqis

Saddam Hussein

At the beginning of 2003 Iraq was ruled by Saddam Hussein, a sixty-six-year-old dictator who had been in power since 1979. Saddam had a well-deserved reputation for extreme brutality toward anyone who represented the slightest threat to his power. Potential rivals were quickly imprisoned or executed—according to some reports, by Saddam himself.

Up until 1990, however, Saddam was considered an ally of the United States. During his eight-year war with neighboring Iran in the 1980s, America supplied Iraq with military help. All that changed, however, in 1990 when Saddam invaded oil-rich Kuwait. An international military coalition led by President George H.W. Bush then mounted an attack that expelled Iraqi forces from Kuwait and greatly weakened Saddam's army.

Saddam, however, remained in power after the Gulf War. At war's end he had agreed to periodic weapons inspections supervised by the United Nations. In 1998, after he had violated the terms of that agreement, U.S. and British warplanes began bombing suspected weapons facilities. War appeared imminent again in 2002 when the United States and Britain warned that Saddam was amassing weapons of mass destruction.

Shortly after coalition troops invaded Iraq in March 2003, Saddam went into hiding. He was not captured until December 2003, when he was pulled out of an underground hiding place near his hometown of Tikrit. From there he was transferred to Iraqi legal custody and was expected to eventually face criminal charges for his actions while president of Iraq.

became willing to take up arms against the coalition. The insurgents killed and wounded soldiers with snipers and attacked convoys with rocket-propelled grenades. By far their most deadly tactic, though, was exploding homemade bombs on streets and roads where coalition troops traveled.

Responding to the danger, the coalition sent out frequent patrols to rout out their attackers from the general Iraqi population. But since few coalition soldiers spoke enough Arabic to be able to distinguish the guilty from the innocent, all Iraqis found in the area of an attack—sometimes hundreds of them—were often arrested and sent off to prison, where their guilt or innocence would supposedly be sorted out later.

The influx of prisoners had to be kept somewhere and, despite its sinister reputation, the huge prison complex at Abu Ghraib seemed the most logical choice. The prison had been stripped bare by looters in April, but coalition authorities decided to return it to its original function. Cells were cleaned and repaired, floors were tiled, and toilets and showers added. By June 2003, just a few months after Saddam was deposed, Abu Ghraib was open again—this time as a U.S. military prison called the Baghdad Central Correctional Facility.

An Unfamiliar Mission

That same month, despite having no prior experience managing prisons, Brigadier General Janis Karpinski of the 800th Military Police Brigade was put in charge of all Iraq's military prisons. Her command included three large jails, eight battalions, as well as a total of thirty-four hundred reservists. Like Karpinski, very few of the soldiers under her command had ever worked in a real prison. Their lack of experience and worsening morale contributed to a tense atmosphere developing inside Abu Ghraib in the late summer and fall of 2003.

Although the MPs (military police) were poorly trained for their new jobs, they were responsible for thousands of prisoners. In addition to being untrained for their assignment, many of the MPs of the 800th did not want to be in Iraq at all. Before the war began, some Bush administration officials had predicted that the majority of coalition troops would be able to leave Iraq by September. The strength of the insurgency, however, made those predictions obsolete. When the men and women of the 800th were told they would not be returning home soon and that their mission had been enlarged to manage the entire Iraqi penal system, many were frustrated and unhappy.

The situation at Abu Ghraib was unlikely to improve anyone's mood. The prison was becoming terribly overcrowded, as more prisoners arrived every day. In addition to the overcrowding the prison was right in the middle of a war zone, contrary to army regulations. Snipers in the palm trees around the prison often fired on U.S. soldiers. At night there were gun battles between the guard towers and armed Iraqis in surrounding neighborhoods. Improvised

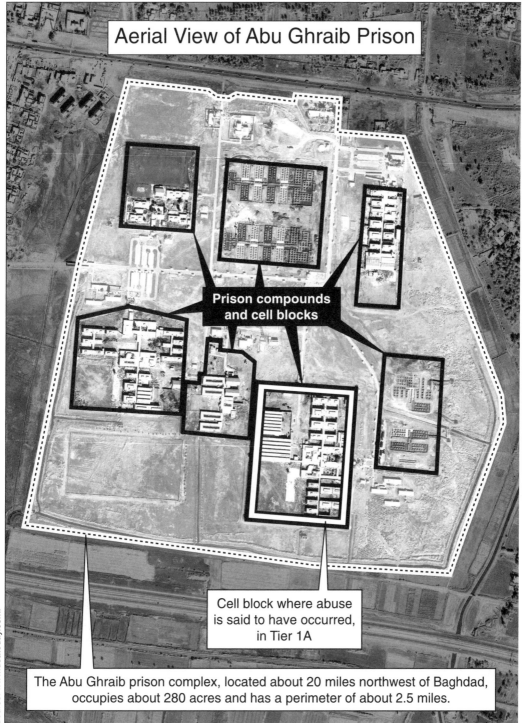

Aerial View of Abu Ghraib Prison

Prison compounds and cell blocks

Cell block where abuse is said to have occurred, in Tier 1A

The Abu Ghraib prison complex, located about 20 miles northwest of Baghdad, occupies about 280 acres and has a perimeter of about 2.5 miles.

An American soldier leads an Iraqi prisoner to a temporary prison camp after a raid near Tikrit. Several of the 270 detainees were members of the Iraqi military.

bombs killed and maimed U.S. soldiers who used the highway that ran past the prison. Meanwhile, countless mortar attacks on the prison killed and wounded guards and prisoners alike.

The stress level on guards at Abu Ghraib steadily increased that summer as their jobs grew more and more difficult. As the insurgency became more deadly, the prison population swelled and the inclination to release even innocent prisoners declined. A typical incident involving fifty-seven Iraqis caught up in a sweep and sent to Abu Ghraib illustrates one reason why innocent prisoners were not released. Although only two of the prisoners were determined to possibly have intelligence value, a general declined to authorize the release of the other fifty-five. He is reported to have defended his actions by saying, "I don't care if they are innocent; if we release them, they'll go out and tell their friends we're after them."[11]

Meanwhile, day after day, the temperature soared well past the one-hundred-degree mark. Stressed both physically and mentally, and under constant threat of at-

tack, some of the guards stopped thinking of Iraqis as the people they had come to free. Instead many began to regard nearly every Iraqi civilian as the enemy.

A Worsening Situation

During that blazing hot summer the attacks on coalition soldiers became more frequent and more deadly. Yet, at the same time, no weapons of mass destruction had been found and Saddam's whereabouts were unknown. A series of terrorist bombings in

American soldiers secure an area in Baghdad after an insurgent's car bomb killed an Iraqi official and three other people.

August only increased the frustration level. A huge bomb early in the month nearly obliterated the Jordanian embassy. Then insurgents struck the UN headquarters in Baghdad with a massive explosion that killed the chief UN envoy to Iraq and twenty-two others.

The bad news was hurting Bush and the mission in Iraq—this was not how the war had been predicted to go. Some in the administration had insisted that grateful Iraqis would greet the coalition as liberators, but clearly this was not the case. The violent situation threatened the success of the war—not only from a military standpoint, but also from a political one.

At the higher levels of command there was an uncomfortable feeling that the situation was careening out of control. The insurgency threatened the reconstruction of Iraq that had been scheduled to follow Saddam's removal. In response, Defense Secretary Rumsfeld decided that it was time to "get tough"[12] with Iraqis in the prison system who were suspected of being insurgents. After all, the coalition had almost no information on who they were or how they operated. If the insurgents were to be stopped and the reconstruction put back on track, such information could be vital.

The desperation to get better information to stop the carnage was keenly felt by soldiers and officers at Abu Ghraib. "There was extraordinary pressure being put on MI [military intelligence] from every angle to get better info," recalls Karpinski. "Where is Saddam? Find Sad-

dam. And we want the weapons of mass destruction."[13]

Changing the Focus

One of the first steps in the new "get tough" approach was to send for Major General Geoffrey Miller, commander of the detention center at the Guantánamo naval base in Cuba. Guantánamo was the place where suspected terrorists from Afghanistan and elsewhere were taken to be interrogated. From August 31 to September 9, 2003, Miller visited detention facilities in Iraq. His stated mission was to show prison officials which interrogation techniques might be used to "break down" prisoners (that is, make them talk) more quickly. Miller urged the commanders of prisons in Iraq to focus more on interrogating prisoners and less on traditional prison functions, such as monitoring prisoners and making sure they did not escape.

In order to make the whole interrogation process more efficient, Miller recommended that military intelligence officers be put in charge of the interrogation facilities at Abu Ghraib and elsewhere. Intelligence officers had a different mission than ordinary soldiers—their main job was to find out information about the enemy. Miller briefed prison commanders on the techniques Guantánamo guards used on prisoners before their interrogations. Although guards normally do not assist in interrogations, the guards at Guantánamo had actively helped out interrogators. They rewarded prisoners who provided useful

General Miller's Visit to Abu Ghraib

In early September 2003, Major General Geoffrey Miller, commander of the military prison at Guantánamo Bay, Cuba, visited Abu Ghraib prison. In an article entitled "Pressure at Iraqi Prison Detailed," the newspaper USA Today *noted the apparent impact of that visit.*

"Seeking to shape up the intelligence-gathering at Abu Ghraib, the Bush administration ordered Army Maj. General Geoffrey Miller, commander of the military prison at Guantánamo Bay, Cuba, to examine the prison in Iraq. Miller . . . recommended that some of the same techniques used to break al-Qaeda fighters at Guantánamo be applied to prisoners in Iraq. . . .

Miller has vehemently denied encouraging abusive treatment. But the report he produced from his initial tour of the Iraqi prison makes clear he wanted guards and military intelligence officers to work together on inmates in a coordinated fashion to maximize the results of interrogations.

Regardless of Miller's intended impact on Abu Ghraib, two facts emerge from the documents: Discipline did not improve in the fall of 2003; if anything, it deteriorated. And harsh treatment of a limited number of inmates became a regular occurence."

Major General Geoffrey Miller pressured officials at Abu Ghraib to employ more aggressive interrogation methods.

information and punished those who did not. Miller felt that the same process could be used at Abu Ghraib.

Miller hammered home the message that the entire detention process should be designed to pressure inmates to provide information. As he explained to Karpinski that September, "You're going to see. We have control and [the prisoners] know it."[14] Perhaps the first evidence of that new policy being put into operation was a cable sent by Lieutenant General Ricardo Sanchez, the senior military commander in Iraq, on September 14. In the cable to his boss at U.S. Central Command, Sanchez listed a group of more aggressive interrogation methods he planned to authorize immediately. These included most of the tactics Miller suggested.

Dealing with Prisoners of War

In essence, what Miller was proposing was that techniques previously used on captured terrorists now be used on suspected Iraqi insurgents. There were some important and controversial differences between the people being held at Abu Ghraib and the people being held at facilities in Afghanistan and Guantánamo Bay, Cuba, however. The treatment of detainees during wartime is a complicated subject, made especially more controversial during the war on terror. Prisoners of war, known as POWs, are protected under international laws called the Geneva Conventions. The most important of these were signed in Geneva, Switzerland, after World War II. Be-

cause atrocities against POWs have been so common in the past, the laws were written with the intent of holding nations to more humane standards. Murder, mutilation, cruel treatment, and torture of POWs are clearly against the law. Violations of personal dignity, including humiliating and degrading treatment, are also forbidden. By setting these standards, it was hoped that those who might be tempted to abuse helpless prisoners would choose not to if they knew their actions might one day be punished. The laws state that anyone accused of violating the Geneva Conventions will be brought before the International Court of Justice.

The United States had always been one of the conventions' strongest backers. Like most nations of the world, the United States signed the conventions because it was something a country could do to protect its own captured soldiers. By agreeing beforehand to treat the POWs it held humanely, the United States made it less likely that future enemies would commit atrocities against American soldiers.

The issue of treating POWs humanely, however, began to blur after the terrorist attacks of September 11, 2001. Many Americans, both inside and outside the Bush administration, believed that suspected terrorists did not deserve the protections of international law. It was argued that those who receive protection from the Geneva Conventions must be soldiers of a national military who fight in uniform—terrorists, it was said, do not fight for legitimate armies or wear distinguishable uniforms. For this and other reasons, many people argued that the

Some Americans argue that detainees captured during the war on terror should be treated as terrorists, who are not protected under the Geneva Conventions.

terrorists that had been detained in the war on terror did not count as POWs and thus did not have to be treated in accordance with the Geneva Conventions.

Moreover, the danger that suspected terrorists posed to society was said to be so great that all available tools should be used to get them to reveal details of their plans. The term for such information is "intelligence," and the war on terrorism was said to require good intelligence if the terrorists were to be defeated. Getting such information, however, often required controversial

rough treatment. Cofer Black, former head of the CIA Counterterrorist Center told a joint hearing of Congress in September 2002 that the war on terror required tougher methods in order to properly deal with suspected terrorists. "There was a before 9/11, and there is an after 9/11," he said. "After 9/11, the gloves came off."[15] Consequently, the United States began meting out harsh treatment to suspected terrorists in Afghanistan and elsewhere—treatment that fell outside the bounds of what was allowable under the Geneva Conventions and other international laws. When international complaints about the harsh treatment of detainees from Afghanistan surfaced in 2002, Rumsfeld dismissed them as of little importance. He believed that critics did not understand the significance of the information to be gathered from terrorists or the danger that their organization presented.

The situation in Iraq, however, was supposed to be different. Because, in the beginning at least, the Iraqis battling against the coalition were thought to be remnants of Saddam's army, the Bush administration agreed that the Geneva Conventions applied fully. Iraqis fighting against the invasion of their own country were not exactly terrorists. Unfortunately, the American military police assigned to guard prisoners at Abu Ghraib knew little about the Geneva Conventions. With forces stretched thin, training soldiers in the Geneva Conventions had not been a high priority for military planners.

Given the stressful situation at Abu Ghraib and the lack of training of the soldiers asked to use the techniques imported from other detention facilities, there was considerable danger they would not be able to stay within the very delicate confines of the rules—and that prisoners would end up being abused.

Chapter Two

Tales of Torture

B y the fall of 2003 the growing Iraqi insurgency led to a renewed focus on the interrogation of Iraqi detainees. But the emphasis on getting intelligence that might save coalition lives also led to increased use of cruelty and torture by poorly trained guards at Abu Ghraib. Meanwhile, the reality of what was taking place inside the prison proved far different from the reality presented to the outside world by American military and government figures.

Miller's changes to the interrogation process appear to have been put into practice almost immediately. In early October 2003, a few weeks after his visit, control of Iraq's prisons was turned over to military intelligence officers. These officers, as well as officers from the Central Intelligence Agency and even private contractors hired by the Defense Department, began overseeing the interrogations of prisoners at Abu Ghraib and elsewhere. Their most pressing need was to get information about the growing insurgency. With that aim in mind, the entire detention process was considered a prelude to an effective interrogation. Consequently, military police and guards began taking orders from interrogators. This was highly unusual—normally, military police and guards take orders from officers in military police units. The unorthodox situation would prove to have far-reaching consequences.

Mysterious Questioners

The interrogators had a different set of priorities than the military police and guards, and they were accountable to an entirely different set of superiors. As far as many of them were concerned, their

American soldiers lead an Iraqi detainee to an interrogation room at Abu Ghraib.

guards asked interrogators to identify themselves, they sometimes gave phony names. Sergeant Javal S. Davis, one of the military policemen later accused of abuses, recalls receiving answers like "I'm Special Agent John Doe" or "I'm Special Agent in Charge James Bond."[16]

The interrogators' reluctance to identify themselves indicated that what was going on inside the prison was not in accordance with the standard procedures used in previous wars. But it also confused soldiers who were not always sure whom they should be taking orders from. The secrecy and the difficulty of knowing whether an order was legitimate led to an atmosphere where the bounds of acceptable behavior were unclear. In the end an "anything goes" attitude prevailed among some of the guards.

Investigative reporter Seymour Hersh noted that the chain of command at Abu Ghraib was so murky that interrogators and other mysterious figures who gave orders were sometimes compared to ghosts:

It was not clear who was who, even to Brigadier General Janis Karpinski, then the commander of the 800th Military Police Brigade and the officer ostensibly in charge. "I thought most of the civilians there were interpreters, but there were some civilians that I didn't know," Karpinski told me. "I called them the disappearing ghosts. I'd seen

mission was to extract information from the detainees in any way they could. The interrogators did not operate openly. They often covered up their name tags or the insignia that showed their rank, indicating that they did not want to be identified. Others wore only civilian clothes and removed their name tags inside the prison. When military police or

Abu Ghraib Prison: The Chain of Command

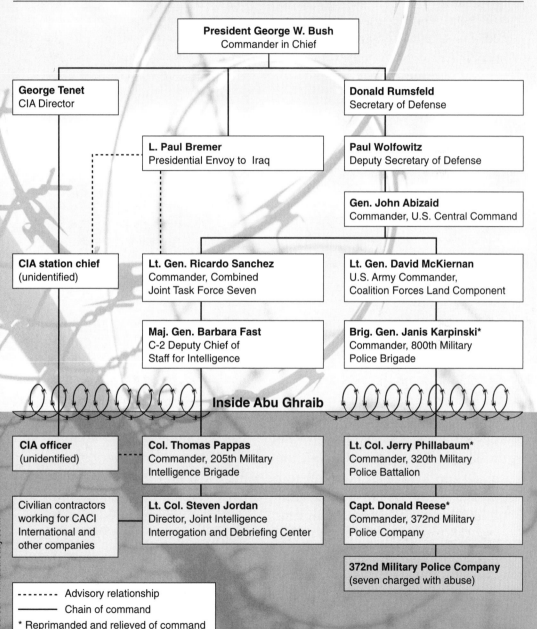

★ ★ ★ ★ ★ **Top Administration, Military, and Intelligence Command** ★ ★ ★ ★ ★

President George W. Bush
Commander in Chief

George Tenet
CIA Director

Donald Rumsfeld
Secretary of Defense

L. Paul Bremer
Presidential Envoy to Iraq

Paul Wolfowitz
Deputy Secretary of Defense

Gen. John Abizaid
Commander, U.S. Central Command

CIA station chief
(unidentified)

Lt. Gen. Ricardo Sanchez
Commander, Combined
Joint Task Force Seven

Lt. Gen. David McKiernan
U.S. Army Commander,
Coalition Forces Land Component

Maj. Gen. Barbara Fast
C-2 Deputy Chief of
Staff for Intelligence

Brig. Gen. Janis Karpinski*
Commander, 800th Military
Police Brigade

Inside Abu Ghraib

CIA officer
(unidentified)

Col. Thomas Pappas
Commander, 205th Military
Intelligence Brigade

Lt. Col. Jerry Phillabaum*
Commander, 320th Military
Police Battalion

Civilian contractors
working for CACI
International and
other companies

Lt. Col. Steven Jordan
Director, Joint Intelligence
Interrogation and Debriefing Center

Capt. Donald Reese*
Commander, 372nd Military
Police Company

372nd Military Police Company
(seven charged with abuse)

- - - - - - - - Advisory relationship
————— Chain of command
* Reprimanded and relieved of command

them once in a while at Abu Ghraib and then I'd see them months later.... "The mysterious civilians," she said, were "always bringing in somebody for interrogation or waiting to collect somebody going out." Karpinski added that she had no idea who was operating in her prison system.[17]

From Maryland to the Middle East

There was plenty of confusion and unprofessional behavior at Abu Ghraib in the fall of 2003, and the members of the 372nd Military Police Company found themselves in the thick of it. A reserve unit from Maryland, the 372nd was sent to guard prisoners at Abu Ghraib. Their duty station included the cellblock known as Tier 1 or, as it was also called, "the hard site."[18] It was the part of the prison where detainees thought most likely to have important information about the insurgency were held.

The 372nd arrived at Abu Ghraib just as control of the prison was turned over to interrogators. They received only two days of on-the-job training from the unit they were replacing. That training did not include any information on how prisoners of war should be treated under the Geneva Conventions.

The 372nd soon found itself under a great deal of pressure—both from Iraqi detainees and from their superiors. When they first began work at the prison, they had only two hundred captives to watch over. But that number soared to as many as sixteen hundred after a series of deadly

roadside bombings caused the coalition to arrest more and more Iraqis as suspects. Once likely suspects were brought to Abu Ghraib for interrogation, they were given rough treatment—particularly those brought to Tier 1. Both military policemen and prison guards there have testified that they were asked to "soften up" prisoners before interrogations. They were told, "Loosen this guy up for us" or "Make sure he has a bad night."[19]

"Rape Rooms and Torture Chambers"

The harsh treatment of detainees conflicted with public statements being made by American officials. In October, Bush announced to the world that "Iraq is now free of rape rooms and torture chambers."[20] At about the same time, General Karpinski told a reporter for the television show *60 Minutes* that prisoners were getting the best care available. Karpinski even bragged that "Living conditions now are better in prison than at home. At one point we were concerned that they wouldn't want to leave."[21]

Meanwhile, inside parts of Abu Ghraib, some Iraqi detainees were experiencing a different kind of reality. Their sworn statements (made later as part of an army investigation into criminal behavior at the prison) indicate that Abu Ghraib was not the model facility that some claimed.

The worst abuses that took place at Abu Ghraib occurred in an area known as Tier 1. Statements from prisoners held captive in that area of Abu Ghraib report that

American soldiers guard a detention area at Abu Ghraib. Inside the prison, many prisoners were routinely subjected to abuse as part of the interrogation process.

most were stripped naked upon arrival. Then they were repeatedly humiliated in front of each other and American soldiers, both men and women. There were frequent and severe beatings as well as threats of death and sexual assault if they did not provide interrogators with the information they were looking for.

Mohanded Juma, an Iraqi detainee, recalls his first few days in Tier 1 in his sworn testimony:

They stripped me from my clothes ... after a short period of time, approximately at two at night, the door opened and Grainer [Specialist Charles Graner]

Although the U.S. government denies authorizing the use of working military dogs at Abu Ghraib, photos like this one show Iraqi detainees being intimidated by a dog handled by an American soldier.

was there. He cuffed my hands behind my back and he cuffed my feet and he took me to the shower room. . . . Then Grainer and another man . . . [who] was young and tall came into the room. They threw pepper in my face and the beating started. This went on for half an hour. And then he started beating

me with a chair until the chair was broken. After that, they started choking me. At the time I thought I was going to die, but it's a miracle I lived. And then they started beating me again. They concentrated on beating me in my heart until they got tired from beating me. They took a little break from beating me and then they started kicking me very hard with their feet until I passed out.[22]

In addition to beatings, threats of sexual abuse and humiliation were made frequently. Ameen Sa'eed Al-Sheikh, detainee No. 151362, was arrested on October 7, 2003, and arrived at Tier 1 the next day. Guards told him he would soon wish he was dead but they would make sure that did not happen. After the soldiers stripped him, says Al-Sheikh, "One of them told me he would rape me. He drew a picture of a woman [on] my back and made me stand in [a] shameful position holding my buttocks."[23] Other prisoners were forced to wear women's underwear, masturbate, or simulate homosexual acts in front of female soldiers and inmates.

Cruelty and Degradation

Sometimes it appeared that guards were simply amusing themselves in the cruelest ways they could think of. Some naked prisoners were ridden like animals, fondled by female "soldiers or forced to retrieve food their guards had thrown in the toilet. They forced us to walk like dogs on our hands and knees," said inmate Hiadar Sabar Abed Miktub al-Aboodi. "And we had to bark like a dog, and if we didn't do that they started hitting us hard on our face and

Torturing for the Greater Good

For a book called The Politics of Pain: Torturers and Their Masters, *Herbert C. Kelman wrote a chapter that sought to explain why humans throughout history have been so easily persuaded to torture others. Kelman, a social psychologist and author, believes that most torturers must become convinced that their actions are part of a greater cause. Only then can they operate without feelings of guilt. Kelman's description of typical torturers can be applied to those committing abuses at Abu Ghraib:*

"They have come to share the view of the authorities that the task they are engaged in serves a high purpose that transcends any moral scruples they might bring to the situation. They have come to see themselves as playing an important part in an effort to protect the state: to ensure its security and continued integrity, to maintain law and order, or to keep alive the fundamental values of the state that are being subjected to a merciless onslaught by ruthless enemies who are intent on destroying it. This view of the purpose of the torture project as part of a noble effort, in which the perpetrators are prepared to play their role despite any more reservations and feelings of repugnance they might have, greatly enhances the legitimacy of the enterprise."

chest with no mercy. After that, they took us to our cells, took the mattresses out and dropped water on the floor and they made us sleep on our stomachs on the floor with the bags on our head and they took pictures of everything."[24]

Another Iraqi, Abd Alwhab Youss, was stripped and then beaten after a broken toothbrush was found in his cell. He was accused of trying to make a weapon out of the toothbrush. Youss was taken to a room where five soldiers worked him over. He was beaten with a broom and at one point his head was held in a pool of urine on the floor. While all this was happening another soldier was yelling at him through a loudspeaker.

Still other abuses occurred in November when a number of detainees rioted in protest against their mistreatment. As reported by The *New Standard,* immediately after the riot fourteen Iraqi men were stripped naked and brought into a corridor beneath the cell of a female inmate named Um Taha.

"The soldiers made them all stand on one leg," Um Taha recounted. "Then they kicked them to make them fall to the ground." She said that [a] female American soldier . . . was dancing around laughing while using a rubber glove to snap the detainees on their genitals. "The soldiers also made all the men lay on the ground face down spread their legs, then men and women soldiers alike kicked the detainees between their legs."[25]

Two American soldiers grin behind a pile of naked and hooded Iraqi prisoners.

"Because I Wanted to Pray"

Some guards took special pleasure in ridiculing the prisoners' Islamic religion. When prisoners held their Korans out of their cell bars to read because the light was too dim inside their cells, some soldiers would hit them. Although Iraqi detainee Ameen Sa'eed Al-Sheik had a broken leg, one of the soldiers kept twisting his bad leg in order to force him to curse Islam. The pain was so great that he finally

Sex, Shame, and Self-Respect

In an article for Salon *magazine called "American Torture, American Porn," Alessandro Camon focuses on the sexual games played with prisoners at Abu Ghraib. He believes they were an important part of an interrogation process designed to destroy detainees' self-respect:*

"When power is exercised in such an extreme, absolute form as torture, it literally dehumanizes those it's exercised upon. And they know it. Stripped of rights, of the ability to trust a fellow human being, and most importantly, of self-respect, they lose the very sense of who they are. The identity of the torture victim can never be the same again.

That's why sexual torture is central to the experience. The emasculation of men, the degradation of women, turns them into something they no longer recognize as themselves. Torture is largely the business of creating shame. . . . An instinctive understanding of the task can be evinced by the acts of the American torturers. They were aiming to hurt the Arab man where it hurts most—in his masculine pride. There was hardly a more explicit way to do it than to strip him naked and capture him . . . as a pathetic loser, writhing on the floor or engaging in simulated sexual acts on command, while American men and women pose next to him with a grin and a thumbs-up."

---

complied with the soldier's wish. Next, he was ordered to thank Jesus that he was still alive. When the soldier asked him if he believed in anything, Al-Sheikh answered that he believed in Allah. The soldier replied, "I believe in torture and I will torture you."[26]

Inmates were treated particularly roughly during Ramadan, the Muslim holy month when all practicing Muslims fast during daylight hours. At Abu Ghraib's Tier I in November 2003, Ramadan was a brutal time for the prisoners. After fasting all day, prisoners were often denied food at night. But the withholding of food was not the worst of their ordeals. To cite one example, Kasim Mehaddi Hilas, detainee No. 151108, made the mistake of asking a guard what time it was:

He [Specialist Graner] cuffed my hands with irons behind my back to the metal of the window, to the point my feet were off the ground and I was hanging there for about 5 hours just because I asked about the time, because I wanted to pray. And then they took all my clothes and he took the female underwear and he put it over my head. After he released me from the window, he tied me to my bed until before dawn. . . . He prohibited me from eating food that night, even though I was fasting that day. Grainer and the other two soldiers were taking pictures of everything they did to me. I don't know if they took a picture of me [then] because they beat me so bad I lost consciousness after an hour or so.[27]

Iraqi detainee Thaar Salman Dawod witnessed an assault on two young boys during the first days of Ramadan. "They came with two boys naked and they were cuffed together face to face and Grainer was beating them and a group of guards were watching and taking pictures from top to bottom and there were three female soldiers laughing at the prisoners."[28] Kasim Mehaddi Hilas, another detainee who made a sworn statement, testified that he

Iraqi women were also held at Abu Ghraib. Some have testified that they experienced the same degree of abuse and humiliation as the male prisoners.

witnessed at least two sexual assaults of children during this time. One of them was of a boy of about fifteen who was raped by a male army translator while a female soldier looked on and snapped pictures.

Abuse Was Not Universal

Of course, not all—or even most—guards abused prisoners. The MPs who abused prisoners most often worked at night while their supervisors were absent. That may explain why the guards who worked the late shift were the most feared by prisoners. A common theme in detainees' statements was that the day shift would bring them their clothes, while the night shift would strip them naked and begin tormenting them again.

Further evidence that not all guards were to blame came from a detainee named Mustafa Jassim Mustafa. After describing a series of sickening abuses (including guards urinating on prisoners and beating them senseless) in a sworn statement to investigators, Mustafa made a point of emphasizing that most of the guards he knew were respected and liked by the prisoners.

In an article published in the *New Yorker,* Seymour Hersh provides a memorable example of an American officer who refused to abuse prisoners. Hersh told of a captain in a military police unit who was asked by an intelligence officer to have his MPs keep a group of detainees awake around the clock until they began talking. When the captain refused, a high-ranking military intelligence officer came to him and asked him again to explain why his men could not help out by keeping detainees awake.

"How?" asked the captain. "You've received training on that, but my soldiers don't know how to do it. And when you ask an eighteen-year-old kid to keep someone awake, and he doesn't know how to do it, he's going to get creative."[29] Because of the captain's stand, his group of MPs did not get involved in abusing prisoners.

Humiliation in Pictures

Those MPs who did abuse detainees, however, were successful at humiliating and intimidating prisoners. One detainee named Abdou Hussain Saad Faleh testified that there were times he was so terrified that he could not go to sleep, no matter how exhausted he was. The inmates' loss of human dignity was also notable. Hussein Mohssein Mata Al-Zayiadi, a devout Muslim, felt so humiliated by being forced to masturbate in front of female soldiers and other inmates that he claimed he no longer wanted to live. "I was trying to kill myself but I didn't have any way of doing it,"[30] he later told an investigator.

Although humiliation and intimidation were products of the interrogations at Abu Ghraib, valuable intelligence was not. Military officials would later concede that very little useful information was gained from the detainees at Abu Ghraib. One of the many tragedies of the whole scandal is that, despite all the suffering involved, little

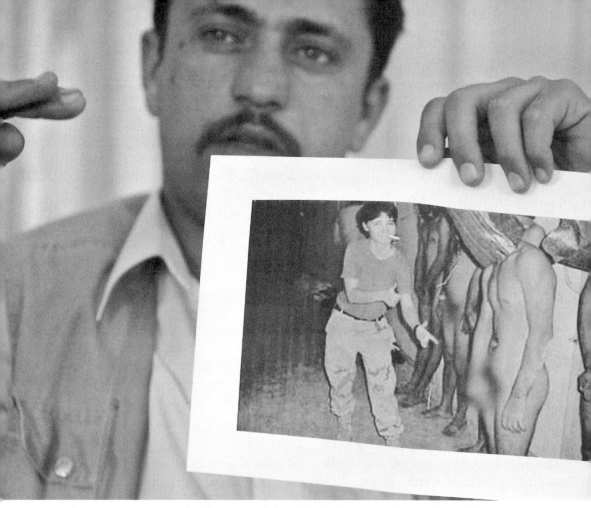

A former Iraqi prisoner holds up a widely published picture of himself and fellow inmates who were abused by American guards.

seems to have been learned about the insurgency.

But perhaps the most lasting effect of the interrogations at Abu Ghraib will be the images they produced. As the world learned, the guards at Abu Ghraib took many photographs. Perhaps they were amusing themselves or saving the photos as memorabilia of their tour of duty. But some observers think that cameras were purposely used at Abu

Ghraib in order to impress on prisoners that their humiliation would be unending unless they cooperated with interrogators. Otherwise the pictures might even be released to the prisoners' friends and relatives, thus deepening their shame. Whether or not the cruelty was indeed that purposeful, the photographs taken at Abu Ghraib became the single greatest factor in exposing the abuses to the world.

Chapter Three

A Scandal Breaks

International human rights organizations, as well as individual soldiers troubled by incidents they witnessed, attempted to alert authorities to the abuses taking place at Abu Ghraib in late 2003 and early 2004. Although the army knew about the abuses by January and conducted an investigation, little substantive action had been taken by April 2004. Few people outside of Iraq had ever heard of Saddam's infamous prison until the images of prisoners being abused suddenly showed up in their newspapers and on their television screens. At that point the world reacted with horror and outrage.

Hints of Disaster

Complaints about prisoners being abused were registered almost as soon as Abu Ghraib reopened. One of the first hints that the prison might be in violation of international standards came from the human rights organization Amnesty International. In July 2003, the organization reported that released prisoners from Abu Ghraib complained of extreme heat while housed in tents, insufficient water, inadequate washing facilities, open trenches for toilets, and no change of clothes—even after two months of detention. For these reasons, Amnesty International criticized the U.S. military for subjecting Iraqis to "cruel, inhumane or degrading"[31] conditions. They also complained that detainees were forced to wear hoods for long periods of time, were deprived of sleep, or forced to remain in painful positions for hours at a time.

The International Committee of the Red Cross also was aware of prisoner-related problems in Iraq. The Red

Although several humanitarian groups expressed concern over the treatment of Iraqi detainees at Abu Ghraib, the U.S. government was slow to implement any improvements.

Cross monitors the behavior of governments at war to ensure that they abide by the terms of the Geneva Conventions. In that role the group conducts unannounced inspections of prisons in war zones. A month after two unannounced inspections of Abu Ghraib in October 2003—visits that included a tour of the cell block where the worst abuses were taking place—the Red Cross complained in writing to the military. Although they witnessed prisoners being kept naked in completely dark and empty concrete cells, no corrective action was taken. And, in fact, when the Red Cross delegates requested an explanation from the authorities, they were told that the practice was "part of the process"[32] and would therefore continue. A confidential letter that military officials sent to the Red Cross explained that many Iraqi prisoners were not entitled to the full protections of the Geneva Conventions—a position that conflicted with the Bush administration's public statements that the Geneva Conventions were "fully applicable"[33] in Iraq.

Karpinski would claim later that, despite the serious charges made by the Red Cross that fall, senior officers in Baghdad treated the reports in a lighthearted manner. Meanwhile, the army's response to the Red Cross's November complaint bordered on annoyance. They also told the Red Cross that in the future no-notice inspections would not be permitted at the site—all inspections would have to be scheduled in advance.

That may help explain Abu Salem's recollection of a Red Cross visit in January

2004. Salem was a forty-one-year-old Iraqi who spent six months in Abu Ghraib before being released. He claimed that although the detainees in his wing were kept naked all the time, the night before the Red Cross visit they were given new clothes. "They told us that if we complained to the Red Cross about our treatment we would be kept in jail forever," said Salem. "They said they would never let us out."[34]

Warnings from Within

Members of human rights organizations were not alone in being troubled by what was going on inside Abu Ghraib that fall. Some within the army itself were raising concerns. The highest ranking officer to do so was Major General Donald Ryder. His report on Iraq's prison systems was released on November 5, 2003. Although Ryder found that Abu Ghraib was overcrowded and lacked basic sanitation and medical facilities, he differed from the Red Cross in that he saw no evidence of prisoner abuse. Ryder may have missed the abuses because his assignment was to study the capabilities of the prison system—not to inspect any one specific prison.

However, Ryder identified a major problem that would soon become glaringly evident—the role of the military police in Iraqi prisons was not clearly defined. MPs seemed responsible for two things. As prison guards, they were supposed to help make prisons run safely and efficiently. But they also seemed to be assisting interrogators in squeezing information out of cap-

tives. Ryder did not think the two roles were compatible. Soldiers assigned duty as prison guards are usually not part of the interrogation teams. It takes years of training and experience to became a good interrogator. None of the prison guards, however, had any training on interrogating prisoners. Despite their lack of training, some of the guards working in Iraq's prisons had worked with interrogators. Before Iraq they had served in Afghanistan, where author Seymour Hersh wrote they had helped "set favorable conditions"[35] for interrogators. That was a nice way of saying that guards helped break the will of prisoners so that they would be more likely to talk to interrogators. But, having untrained nineteen- or twenty-year-old guards administering punishments was a situation that demanded strong supervision. Ryder was concerned enough to call for the establishment of clear procedures. By then, however, it was too late—the worst abuses were already occurring.

Some of the soldiers who observed those abuses tried to alert their superiors. Specialist Matthew Wisdom, for example, questioned the treatment of seven prisoners, who were hooded and bound, that he delivered to Tier 1 at Abu Ghraib. Although those prisoners had been accused of starting a riot in another section of the prison, Wisdom was shocked by the rough treatment they received: "Specialist First Class Snider grabbed my prisoner and threw him into a pile. . . . I do not think it was right to put them in a pile. I saw Staff Sgt Frederick, Sgt Davis, and Corporal Graner walking

Guards at Abu Ghraib prison were encouraged by interrogators to help break the will of prisoners. In this photo, an American soldier beats Iraqi detainees, who are hooded and bound by the hands.

around the pile hitting the prisoners." Wisdom left the area for a few minutes, but on his return he "saw two naked detainees, one masturbating to another. . . . I thought I should just get out of there. I didn't think it was right. . . . I saw Staff Sgt. Frederick walking towards me, and he said, 'Look what these animals do when you leave them alone for two seconds.'"[36]

Wisdom was disgusted by what the guards were forcing the prisoners to do. He told his superiors about what had happened and assumed the matter would be taken care of. "I just didn't want to be part of anything that looked criminal,"[37] he said.

Members of the Detainee Assessment Branch at Abu Ghraib had raised similar concerns. Their job was to screen detainees for possible release. The vast majority of those they dealt with had been found innocent of any activities that threatened the coalition and were about to be set free. As a part of the release process, interrogators often asked prisoners about their treatment while in U.S. custody. The answers they received made them uneasy.

Blowing the Whistle

Immediately after the Abu Ghraib scandal broke, reporter Andrew A. Green attempted to learn more about Specialist Joseph Darby, the soldier who alerted the army to the abuses going on there. Green spoke with Darby's wife in Cumberland, Maryland, and the interview was published in the Baltimore Sun:

"Bernadette Darby, [Joseph's] wife of six years, said she didn't know a thing about her husband's role in uncovering the scandal until a reporter called yesterday. But it sounded like something he would do, she said. 'Whenever he knows something's wrong, he doesn't stand by it,' she said. 'I'm behind him

100 percent.' . . . Joseph Darby wasn't excited to be deployed to Iraq, Bernadette Darby said, because he had recently returned from a tour of duty in the Balkans. But once he got there, he came to believe that the United States needs to be in Iraq. . . .

Bernadette Darby said she is a little nervous about how other military families will react to her husband's role in uncovering the scandal, but she said she is proud of him and would do the same if she were in his situation. 'It sickened me whenever I saw those pictures,' she said. 'Trust me, his whole unit, they're not all like that. The community is in an uproar about it, and it's just—they're not all sick like that.'"

"One guy said he was thrown to the ground and [was] stepped on the head," said one soldier. "That's when I started paying attention to it."[38] They also heard from a woman prisoner who claimed she was repeatedly kicked by a guard. Other prisoners told of electric shocks, of being forced to stand naked while female interrogators made fun of their genitals, and how a group of blindfolded former Iraqi generals were beaten until covered in blood. One prisoner's file included photos of burns inflicted on his body. "We couldn't believe what we were hearing," said one of the soldiers. Concerned that crimes were being committed, the soldiers in the Detainee Assessment Branch passed along what they

heard in the reports to their superiors. "We didn't want people to know that we knew about it and didn't report it,"[39] one soldier explained. Their reports were sent up the chain of command to Karpinski, General Barbara Fast, and a military lawyer. Whether they were read is not known.

A Shocking CD

What is known for certain is that no action was taken until mid-January. That was when a military policeman in the 372nd named Joseph Darby came across a computer CD belonging to Specialist Charles Graner. The CD contained numerous digital photographs of guards taunting naked Iraqi prisoners who were forced to assume humiliating poses. The Iraqis were piled in human pyramids or forced to simulate oral sex or masturbation with each other. At least one photo showed a naked Iraqi being led around with a leash. Another showed an Iraqi standing on a box and connected to electric wires. Some photos showed terrified prisoners being confronted by dogs. There were also pictures of the battered faces of two dead Iraqis.

Darby was shocked by the pictures and felt that someone should know about them. His first action was to anonymously put the disk in an envelope and slide it under the door of a member of the army's criminal investigation division. Later, Darby agreed to testify about what he had seen. In contrast to their response to the written complaints of human rights organizations, the army's reaction to the photos uncovered by Darby was remarkably swift. There was little doubt that the pictures could trigger a public relations disaster—the photos had been passed from computer to computer within the unit and might already be on the Internet. The day after Darby slipped the CD under the door, a criminal investigation was launched. Four days later, a guard leader and a company commander at the prison were suspended from their duties. Karpinski was also quietly suspended. On January 19, 2004, General Ricardo Sanchez, the senior commander in Iraq, ordered a separate, high-level investigation of the 800th Military Police Brigade. Major General Antonio Taguba was named to head that investigation. He and a team of investiga-

tors spent the entire month of February conducting interviews at Abu Ghraib and elsewhere in Iraq.

Crimes amid Chaos

Taguba found a prison in chaos. It was filled beyond capacity while the guards who were supposed to be ensuring order were undertrained, undermanned, and short of the resources to do their job properly. He also discovered that horrific abuses had indeed occurred. He cited numerous examples of "sadistic, blatant, and wanton criminal abuses."[40] These abuses included

This Iraqi prisoner, hooded and standing on a small box, was led to believe he would be shocked if he moved.

"pouring cold water on naked detainees; beating detainees with a broom handle and a chair; threatening male detainees with rape; allowing a military police guard to stitch the wound of a detainee who was injured after being slammed against the wall in his cell; sodomizing a detainee with a chemical light and perhaps a broom stick, and using military working dogs to frighten and intimidate detainees."[41]

The situation was even more appalling when one realized, as Taguba's final report concluded, that the majority of detainees at Abu Ghraib were not guilty of anything other than being in the wrong place at the wrong time. A confidential report given to the White House by the Red Cross noted that military intelligence officers they had talked with had estimated that 70 to 90 percent of the prisoners detained in Iraq had been arrested by mistake. Taguba said that at least 60 percent of the inmates at Abu Ghraib were not deemed a threat, yet, because of a lack of a proper system to release them in a timely manner, many had been kept behind bars indefinitely.

In addition, Taguba had little good to say about what he claimed was the widest range of leadership failings he had ever seen. He was appalled at how poorly prepared the soldiers working in Iraq's prisons had been for their difficult mission, and he attributed that to poor leadership. He recommended that Karpinski and seven military police officers and enlisted men not only be removed from command but formally reprimanded. On February 26, 2004, seventeen military personnel were suspended from their duties, but no details of their crimes were given to the public. On March 20, six low-ranking soldiers were charged with abuses at Abu Ghraib.

General Taguba

Major General Antonio Taguba, the army officer who first investigated the abuses at Abu Ghraib, is a Filipino immigrant whose own father was tortured during World War II. Tomas Taguba was captured by the Japanese and survived the infamous Bataan Death March, a forced march in which between five and eleven thousand Allied soldiers died.

The Taguba family moved to Hawaii from the Philippines when Antonio was eleven years old. After graduating from college at Idaho State in 1972, he joined the U.S. Army. As an officer he rose through the ranks and after twenty-five years of service became a general. During his career, Major General Taguba has been awarded the Distinguished Service Medal, the Legion of Merit, and the Bronze Star. His reputation for honesty and integrity is a likely reason he was chosen to conduct the first investigation into the Abu Ghraib Scandal.

Investigation Remained Secret

Since the Taguba report was classified as secret, its findings were not passed on to the American public. There seems to have been a conscious effort to keep Taguba's

Army major general Antonio Taguba investigated the situation at Abu Ghraib. He blamed a lack of leadership for the cases of sadistic abuse he uncovered.

finding within military circles. No doubt there was concern that the shocking abuses he found would cause an uproar if generally known—both within the United States and the rest of the world.

Even inside the military, knowledge of Abu Ghraib was severely restricted. "Everybody I've talked to said, 'We just didn't know'—not even in the J.C.S. [Joint Chiefs of Staff],"[42] one well-informed former intelligence official reported. The entire investigation was conducted under conditions of unusual secrecy. Although Taguba's superior approved the report on April 6, few of the nation's top military leaders at the Pentagon were aware of the report's explosive findings.

The public comments made by Bush during this time suggest that he, too, had little awareness of the conclusions reached by the Taguba report. During March and April he and other members of his administration made a number of statements celebrating the fact that rape and torture were no longer a feature of Iraqi life. For example, the president told a group of women on March 12, 2004, that, "Every woman in Iraq is better off because the rape rooms and torture chambers of Saddam Hussein are forever closed."[43]

A Bombshell Broadcast

The lid of secrecy over the scandal, however, was about be blown off with a dramatic one-two punch. On April 12 the CBS television news program *60 Minutes II* informed officials at the Pentagon in Washington that they were about to broadcast a story on Abu Ghraib prison—a story that included graphic photographs of guards abusing prisoners. General Richard Meyers, chairman of the Joint Chiefs of Staff, made a hasty call to *CBS News* anchorman Dan Rather requesting that the broadcast be delayed. Meyers claimed that the pictures could incite violence against U.S. troops and might endanger hostages held by Iraqi militants. CBS agreed to delay the broadcast, but on April 28 they ran the story.

The broadcast showed numerous photographs of guards posing next to naked prisoners, as well as shots of prisoners being forced into simulated sex acts. It also mentioned the existence of a picture of a dead Iraqi who appeared to have been badly beaten. One memorable shot, which, for many people, would come to represent the whole Abu Ghraib affair, showed a prisoner standing on a box with electrodes attached to his arms. Reportedly, he was told that if he fell off the box he would be electrocuted. Such methods were used to keep exhausted prisoners from falling asleep while standing up. Another hard-to-forget image showed a guard dog attacking a terrified, naked prisoner. In many of the pictures the Americans were laughing, posing, pointing, or giving the camera a thumbs-up.

A spokesman for the U.S. military in Iraq also spoke during the *60 Minutes* report. Brigadier General Mark Kimmett, deputy director of coalition operations in Iraq, noted that, "If we can't hold ourselves up as an example of how to treat people with dignity and respect, we can't ask that other nations do that to our soldiers."[44] Kimmit did his best to limit the damage to America's image. He said that, if given the opportunity, he would tell the Iraqi people that these actions were reprehensible and not representative of all Americans. He had a similar message for the American people: "Don't judge your army based on the actions of a few."[45]

Initial Reactions

The CBS report was followed a few days later by an article in the *New Yorker* by Seymour Hersh that revealed the findings

In the wake of the Abu Ghraib scandal, a Libyan child participating in a protest holds a sign condemning the United States as a gross violator of human rights.

of the Taguba report. Taken together, the CBS broadcast and Hersh's article unleashed a firestorm of criticism—both within the United States and internationally. Like other international observers, *La Razon,* a newspaper in Madrid, Spain, noted that the damage done went far beyond Iraq: "The authors of these despicable acts have not only degraded Iraqi prisoners; the humiliation has been suffered by the values of freedom and democracy that, theoretically, the forces of the West represent and defend."[46] South Africa's *Business Day* expanded on a similar theme, wondering whether the scandal "may be the end of the assumption that the great democracies of the west are run by men and women of honor. . . . Being taken prisoners by the British or the Americans used to be a guarantee of safety. No

longer."[47] The pictures from Abu Ghraib horrified even America's strongest ally, Britain. "We went to Iraq to get rid of that type of thing, not to do it,"[48] said British prime minister Tony Blair.

Understandably, the harshest condemnations came from the Middle East. In an interview with Ray Suarez of the Public Broadcasting System, Hisham Melhem, a correspondent for the Lebanese newspaper, *As-Safir,* voiced a disgust that was nearly universal in the Arab world:

People were shocked, they were stunned that these abuses were occurring and that the Americans were the perpetrators now. Those who came supposedly to Iraq as liberators ended up as tormentors of those people. The irony is that these abuses were

A Promise by the President

On May 5, 2004, President Bush attempted to address the anger in the Arab world over Abu Ghraib by appearing on Al Arabiya, a twenty-four hour news station based in the Middle East. One of the first questions the reporter asked was how the president thought the scandal would be perceived in the Middle East:

"Terrible. I think people in the Middle East who want to dislike America will use this as an excuse to remind people about their dislike. I think the average citizen will say, this

isn't a country that I've been told about. We're a great country because we're a free country, and we do not tolerate these kind of abuses. . . .

Secondly, it's very important for the people of the Middle East to realize that the troops we have overseas are decent, honorable citizens who care about freedom and peace; that they are working daily in Iraq to improve the lives of the Iraqi citizens, and these actions of a few people do not reflect the nature of the men and women who serve our country."

taking place in Abu Ghraib, the most notorious prison during Saddam's regime, a facility that should have been razed to the ground and in its place built a shrine or memorial to its many victims.[49]

Al-Ahram, a newspaper in Cairo, Egypt, was not alone in predicting that the scandal would ensure Arab hate and distrust of American policies for decades. Ahmed Abu Zeid, a member of Egypt's parliament, warned "that the savage way the Americans dealt with Iraqi prisoners could create generations of [terrorist mastermind Osama] Bin Ladens determined to take revenge and retaliate against America."[50]

Mixed Reactions at Home

President Bush was quick to assure the world that the United States was not practicing torture. "Let me make very clear the position of my government and our country: We do not condone torture," the president said. "I have never ordered torture. I will never torture. The values of this country are such that torture is not a part of our soul and our being."[51] His words did little to put the issue to rest, however. Most Americans reacted with shock and dismay to news of the Iraqi prison scandal. As the shock wore off, controversy erupted. While some people were upset by the evidence suggesting that American soldiers were engaged in torture, others felt that the affair had been blown out of proportion. Two letters, published side by side in *Time* magazine, illustrate how Americans could think

about the scandal in entirely different ways. Ross Edwards of Palatine, Illinois, was appalled by the fact that the abuses at Abu Ghraib put all American soldiers in greater danger while at the same time tarnishing the nation's reputation:

> As a former U.S. soldier who served in Iraq, I am ashamed of the abuse inflicted on Abu Ghraib prisoners by American troops. The actions shown in the photographs were deliberate, and the soldiers' excuse that they were simply following orders is absurd. Every U.S. service member has the right to decline an order that is morally wrong. All the proper training in the world cannot replace a lack of morals. This scandal undermines everything that I and many others did to help the Iraqi people.[52]

Meanwhile, Chase Hoozer of Houston, Texas, spoke for those who believed that the scandal was overblown: "We should be angered by the extensive outrage over Abu Ghraib. It's easy for people to judge soldiers, but I thank them for the job they are doing. They are dealing with fighters who kill Americans without thought or concern. The critics should shut up."[53]

Still others argued that what the photographs depicted was not so much abuse as aggressive hazing or joking. Still others argued that in the new war on terror, the United States owed no apologies. Influential radio talk show host Rush Limbaugh emphatically told his audience of roughly 20 million listeners that what had happened at

Abu Ghraib was no different than a prank at a college fraternity and that it would be a tragedy if soldiers' lives were ruined over it. "I'm talking about people having a good time, these people, you ever heard of emotional release? You [ever] heard of the need to blow some steam off?"[54]

Rumsfeld Under Attack

Perhaps the most visible administration figure in the days after the scandal broke was Defense Secretary Donald Rumsfeld. Rumsfeld quickly came under fire for behavior that suggested he did not consider the issue a high priority. He admitted that he had not read the Taguba report, which had been completed in February, until the first week of May. He had also not looked at the sickening photographs from Abu Ghraib until more than a week after they were shown on *60 Minutes II*. Members of the Senate Intelligence Committee were upset because Rumsfeld had briefed them on the Iraq war on the same day that the *60 Minutes* story ran, yet he had not warned them about the shocking images that he knew were about to be broadcast. Some White House aides complained that, while Rumsfeld had mentioned

Testifying on Capitol Hill in May 2004, Defense Secretary Donald Rumsfeld accepts full responsibility for the Abu Ghraib scandal.

Abu Ghraib to President Bush back in February, he had done so with little sense of urgency.

Rumsfeld also faced tough questions about the possibility of American troops committing murders. One of the more disturbing photos from Abu Ghraib showed a dead body wrapped in cellophane. According to reporter Seymour Hersh, the bruised and battered corpse had been packed in ice until someone decided the best way to dispose of it. After twenty-four hours, men posing as medics placed a fake intravenous needle in one arm, then took the body away to an undisclosed location. One of the guards testified that the dead man's name had never been entered into the prison's inmate-control system. Calls for an explanation by Rumsfeld increased when it was revealed that since September 11 at least twenty-four other prisoners had died while in U.S. custody. "We're not just talking about giving people a humiliating experience," said Senator Lindsay Graham of South Carolina. "We're talking about rape and murder and some very serious charges."[55]

Graham was far from the only lawmaker who wanted answers about Abu Ghraib. Both Democrats and Republicans expressed outrage. On Friday, May 7, Rumsfeld spent an uncomfortable day testifying to Congress about Abu Ghraib. He said he took full responsibility for what happened, but at

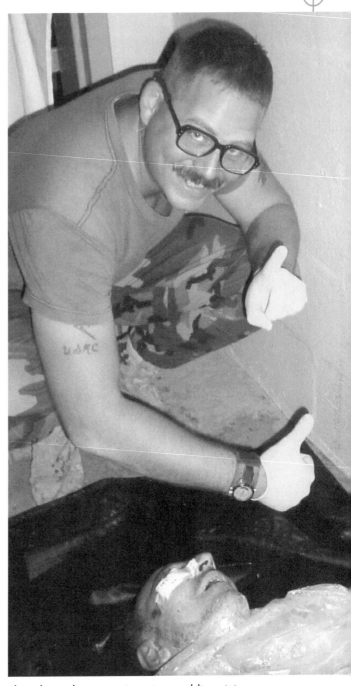

This photo shows an American soldier giving a thumbs-up over the body of a dead prisoner wrapped in cellophane.

the same time he implied that the scandal could have been prevented if someone had stepped forward. "It breaks our hearts," he said at one point, "that someone did not say, 'Wait. Look, this is terrible. We need to do something.'"[56]

A Vow to Find the Truth

President Bush's actions immediately after the scandal broke left little doubt that he thought the matter was of grave concern. He said that the photographs sickened him, and he insisted that the events at Abu Ghraib did not represent the true nature of the American people. He also took the unprecedented step of going on satellite television to broadcast an explanation to the Arab world:

> This is a serious matter. It's a matter that reflects badly on my country. Our citizens in America are appalled by what they saw, just like people in the Middle East are appalled. We share the same deep concerns. And we will

find the truth, we will fully investigate. The world will see the investigation and justice will be served.[57]

Indeed, it became apparent to many observers that the way in which the scandal was handled could serve to salvage some of the damage done, or threaten to make things worse. As one *Washington Post* editorial reluctantly concluded: "Pentagon officials say they will pursue investigations vigorously and that those guilty of crime will be brought to justice. It is essential to the preservation of this country's fundamental values that they do so."[58]

Whether relations with Arab countries could be mended remained to be seen, but the widespread shock and outrage spurred the U.S. government to launch a series of investigations that May. The investigators' findings, it was hoped, would explain whether the atrocities at Abu Ghraib were caused by the actions of a few renegade soldiers—or were evidence of a deeper, more widespread problem.

Chapter Four

Bad Apples— or Bad Policy?

In the days after the Abu Ghraib scandal broke, it was widely believed that the abuses were limited to one particular prison outside Baghdad and were caused by a few rogue soldiers, commonly referred to as a few "bad apples."[59] However, as time passed, it became apparent that abuses had occurred at other U.S. detention facilities elsewhere in the world. It seemed that a changed official policy toward suspected terrorists was one cause of the scandal. New and tougher interrogation techniques intended for use on suspected terrorists came to be used on ordinary Iraqi citizens instead. The use of these techniques elsewhere made it difficult to claim that Abu Ghraib was an aberration. Another important cause of the scandal was a chaotic and unclear prison environment in which soldiers were unsure who was giving orders and supervisors were either un-

aware of soldiers' activity or negligent in seeing that the rules were followed.

A Handful of Troublemakers

During the immediate aftermath of Abu Ghraib, Bush administration officials claimed that the abuses were limited to one prison and were not representative of U.S. policy. In hearings before Congress both General Richard Myers, chairman of the Joint Chiefs of Staff, and his boss Defense Secretary Donald Rumsfeld apologized for what they repeatedly called "the actions of a few"[60] rogue MPs and the military intelligence personnel who spurred them on to commit abuses.

Meanwhile, a senior White House aide told reporters for *Time* magazine that the abuses were unrelated to interrogations at all. Instead, he asserted,

In hearings before Congress, General Richard Myers and Rumsfeld condemned the instances of abuse as the actions of aberrant MPs and interrogators.

it was the work of a few undisciplined MPs egged on by a ringleader who enjoyed abusing helpless Iraqis. "It was the night shift,"[61] the aide claimed. Brigadier General Mark Kimmitt was asked what he would say to the people of Iraq. "This is wrong. This is reprehensible," he replied. "But this is not representative of the 150,000 soldiers that are over here."[62]

Those who believed the abuses were the work of an isolated few were pleased when the Pentagon's inspector general concluded on July 22, 2004, after a study of ninety-four documented cases of prison abuse, that all were aberrations. That prompted statements of relief by some members of Congress. "This senator never doubted for a minute," said Senator Jim Talent of Missouri, "that no senior leader in the United States Army or in the government would tolerate inhumanity or cruelty to prisoners."[63] Talent's opinion was shared by millions of Americans who did not think that the kinds of acts seen at Abu Ghraib would ever be explicitly sanctioned by senior military commanders.

The Torture Memos— Changing the Rules

However, as the scandal was further investigated, it appeared to be much more complicated than originally thought. Indeed, the abuses at Abu Ghraib seemed to be connected to a general change in policy re-garding the treatment of detainees in the war on terror. This suspicion arose when legal documents relating to the war on terror were released by the White House in June 2004. Written by Justice Department lawyers, the documents indicated that the use of techniques that bordered on torture had been considered for use by people at the highest levels of the U.S. government. The media dubbed the documents as the "torture memos"[64] because they appeared to show a government actively searching

Defending Rumsfeld

Following the uproar over the exposure of the Abu Ghraib scandal, many Americans called for Donald Rumsfeld's resignation as secretary of defense. Others, however, said that he was doing a good job. Among Rumsfeld's supporters was Congressman Duncan Hunter, chairman of the House Armed Services Committee:

"Donald Rumsfeld is doing a good job. As Chairman of the House Armed Services Committee, I have found Secretary Rumsfeld to be an effective manager of our military forces in the war on terrorism.

Whether he is an effective leader of our military department, not his friendships on Capitol Hill, should and must be the basis on which he is judged.... The abuses at Abu Ghraib prison, which have resulted in six military personnel being recommended for courts-martial are, in isolation, serious. However, the proposition that Secretary Rumsfeld should drop his focus on the wars in Iraq and Afghanistan and devote all his time to Congressional and media hand-holding, is not acceptable....

Secretary Rumsfeld's military commander in Iraq, General Sanchez, immediately initiated an investigation on January 16, 2004, and announced that investigation to the world media at the same time. The investigation resulted, to-date, with three persons being recommended to the U.S. Army Court Martial Convening Authority for general courts-martial. Simply put, the wheels of Army justice are moving and as the nation knows, will move much quicker than the domestic justice system....

Even Rumsfeld's enemies must concede that the Secretary's strong point is his effectiveness in the war theaters. In war that should be the only thing. We are at war: we need Secretary Rumsfeld."

for ways around the provisions of the Geneva Conventions.

The process seemed to have begun in February 2002 when Bush signed an order declaring that he had the power to suspend the Geneva Conventions when dealing with terrorists. Then, in August 2002, the Justice Department advised White House counsel Alberto Gonzales that torturing terrorism suspects might be legal. Finally, another memo in March 2003 found that "President Bush was not bound by either an international treaty prohibiting torture or by a federal anti-torture law."[65] In essence, the president's lawyers were claiming that in his wartime role as commander in chief the president could ignore laws against torture as he saw fit. These memos sharply departed from former U.S. policy, which stressed the importance of complying with international laws against torture.

Changing the definition of torture greatly expanded the tactics available to interrogators. It was claimed, for example, that inflicting moderate or fleeting pain was not necessarily torture and therefore broke no laws. The author of one memo, Assistant Attorney General Jay S. Bybee, argued that although such actions, while possibly cruel or inhuman, were not really torture. As long as the pain inflicted was of lesser intensity than the pain accompanying serious physical injury or even death, it did not count as torture. In addition, he

Taught to Torture?

On May 24, 2004, Newsweek *magazine published a special report on the root causes of the abuses of the prison scandal. The article noted that the scenes from Abu Ghraib were unlikely to have been the work of rogue soldiers:*

"Indeed, the single most iconic image to come out of the abuse scandal—that of a hooded man standing naked on a box, arms outspread, with wires dangling from his fingers, toes and penis—may do a lot to undercut the administration's case that this was the work of a few criminal MPs. That's because the practice shown in that photo is an arcane torture method known only to veterans of the interrogation trade. 'Was that something that [an MP] dreamed up by herself? Think again,' says Darius Rejali, an expert on the use of torture by democracies. 'That's a standard torture. It's called "the Vietnam." But it's not common knowledge. Ordinary American soldiers did this, but someone taught them.'

Who might have taught them? Almost certainly it was their superiors up the line. Some of the images from Abu Ghraib, like those of naked prisoners terrified by attack dogs or humiliated before grinning female guards, actually portray 'stress and duress' techniques officially approved at the highest levels of the government for use against terrorist suspects."

INTERROGATION RULES OF ENGAGEMENT

Approved approaches for All detainees:

- rect
- .centive
- Incentive Removal
- Emotional Love / Hate
- Fear Up Harsh
- Fear Up Mild
- Reduced Fear
- Pride & Ego Up
- Futility
- We Know All
- Establish Your Identity
- Repetition
- File & Dossier
- Rapid Fire
- Silence

Require CG's Approval:
Requests must be submitted in writing

- Change of scenery down
- Dietary Manip (monitored by med)
- Environmental Manipulation
- Sleep Adjustment (reverse sched)
- Isolation for longer than 30 days
- Presence of Mil Working Dogs
- Sleep Management (72 hrs max)
- Sensory Deprivation (72 hrs max)
- Stress Positions (no longer than 45 min)

Safeguards:
- ~ Techniques must be annotated in questioning strategy
- ~ Approaches must always be humane and lawful
- ~ Detainees will NEVER be touched in a malicious or unwanted manner
- ~ Wounded or medically burdened detainees must be medically cleared prior to interrogation
- ~ The Geneva Conventions apply within CJTF-7

EVERYONE IS RESPONSIBLE FOR ENSURING COMPLIANCE TO THE IROE. VIOLATIONS MUST BE REPORTED IMMEDIATELY TO THE OIC.

The use of the techniques are subjects to the general safeguards as provided as well as specific guidelines implemented by the 205th MI Cdr, FM 34-52, and the Commanding General, CJTF-7

Although interrogators at Abu Ghraib were formally instructed to comply with guidelines for humane treatment, the evidence suggests they were encouraged to disregard them.

claimed that inflicting mental pain or suffering—like pressing a gun to a prisoner's head and threatening to pull the trigger—would qualify as torture only if it resulted in psychological harm that lasted months or years.

In 2002 and 2003 lawyers for the State Department, as well as military lawyers, ex-pressed concerns that memos like Bybee's signalled a drastic and unwise policy change. The criticism of William H. Taft IV, legal adviser for the State Department, was blunt. In a letter to the Justice Department he argued that the Justice Department's advice to the president was deeply flawed and "contrary to the official position of the

United States, the United Nations, and all other states that have considered the issue."[66] Military lawyers opposed the change in policy because it did not provide clear guidance on acceptable tactics. "Once you start telling people it's okay to break the law," said one, "there's no telling where they might stop."[67] Secretary of State Colin Powell, a former soldier who had seen combat in Vietnam, was also skeptical. He sharply disagreed with the notion that the United States could disregard the provisions of the Geneva Conventions under any circumstances.

"Why Is Standing Limited to Four Hours?"

The threat of terrorist attacks on innocent Americans, however, was deemed too serious to fully heed such concerns. Therefore, in late 2002 Rumsfeld approved a list of aggressive interrogation techniques that could be used at the detention facility in Guantánamo Bay. These included stripping prisoners, intimidating them with dogs, subjecting them to twenty-hour interrogations, and forcing them to remain in stressful positions. In one memo an official proposed limiting to four hours the length of time detainees could be forced to stand in one position. A note scrawled in the margin by Rumsfeld shows that he took an active interest in how the techniques were applied. "I stand for 8–10 hours a day," he wrote. "Why is standing limited to four hours?"[68] After these techniques were found to be legal in March

2003, Secretary Rumsfeld then approved a final list of twenty-four interrogation techniques to be used on terrorist suspects at Guantánamo. The methods Rumsfeld authorized included limiting prisoners' food, denying them clothing, subjecting them to body cavity searches, and keeping them awake for as long as ninety-six hours.

According to newspaper reports, those techniques were likely put to use by the CIA in Afghanistan and Guantánamo Bay shortly after they were approved. A December 2002 article on terrorist suspects in Afghanistan in the *Washington Post* shows how detainees there were treated:

> Those who refuse to cooperate inside this secret CIA interrogation center are sometimes kept standing or kneeling for hours, in black hoods or spray-painted goggles, according to intelligence specialists familiar with CIA interrogation methods. At times they are held in awkward, painful positions and deprived of sleep with a 24-hour bombardment of lights— subject to what are known as stress and duress techniques.[69]

The line between torture and interrogation, the *Post* noted, had already begun to blur. While official policy publicly denounced the use of torture, each of the national security officials interviewed for the article defended the use of violence against captives as just and necessary. An official who supervised the capture and transfer of accused terrorists summarized the prevailing attitude. "If you don't violate someone's human rights some of the time," he said, "you probably aren't doing your job."[70]

Treatment during the first few hours of captivity, intended to instill fear and anxiety, could be particularly brutal:

> According to Americans with direct knowledge . . . captives are often "softened up by MPs and U.S. Army Special Forces troops who beat them up and confine them in tiny rooms. The alleged terrorists are commonly blindfolded and thrown into walls,

bound in painful positions, subjected to loud noises and deprived of sleep. The tone of intimidation and fear is the beginning, they said, of a process of piercing a prisoner's resistance.[71]

From Guantánamo to Abu Ghraib

As the Abu Ghraib scandal was further investigated, it seemed likely that the rough techniques approved for interrogators to

The Reuters Incident

In January 2004 three employees of Reuters, an international news agency based in London, were arrested by American soldiers near Fallujah—even though they had no weapons and carried press badges. They were eventually released, but as Greg Mitchell noted in Editor and Publisher, *they were subjected to days of physical and sexual abuse while confined. Their treatment—as well as the use of badges—suggests an organized system of abuse that applied to other prisons beside Abu Ghraib:*

"Bags were alternately placed on their heads and taken off again. Deafening music was played on loudspeakers directly into their ears and they were told to dance around the room. Sometimes when they were doing this, soldiers would shine very bright [flashlights] into their eyes and hit them with the [flashlights]. They were told to lie on the floor and wiggle their backsides in the air to the music. . . .

Soldiers would whisper in their ears, 'One, two, three . . .' and then shout something loudly right beside their ear. All of this went on all night. . . . [One of the Reuters' employees named] Ahmad said he collapsed by morning. [Another named] Sattar said he collapsed after Ahmad and began vomiting. . . .

Ahmad said he was forced to insert a finger into his anus and lick it. He was also forced to lick and chew a shoe. For some of the interrogation, tissue paper was placed in his mouth and he had difficulty breathing and speaking. . . .

Ahmad and Sattar both said that they were given badges with the letter *C* on them. They did not know what the badges meant but whenever they were being taken from one place to another in the base, if any soldier saw their badge they would stop to slap them or hurl abuse."

A U.S. Marine working with a patrol dog conducts vehicle searches at the U.S. Naval base in Guantánamo Bay, Cuba. Interrogators at the Guantánamo prison compound are reported to have used such dogs to intimidate prisoners.

use on terrorists at Guantánamo had found their way to Iraq. Indeed, many of the interrogation techniques used by guards at Abu Ghraib bore a striking resemblance to those that had been used elsewhere. Hooding prisoners and stripping them naked, for example, had been done frequently at Guantánamo and in Afghanistan. The use of dogs to intimidate detainees had also been used at both places and were clearly part of the interrogation process at Abu Ghraib.

Military dog handlers like Sergeant Michael Smith and Sergeant Santos Cardona testified that they were called to Abu Ghraib frequently in December 2003 and January 2004. Normally, the dogs searched for hidden drugs, explosives, and weapons. Their presence at Abu Ghraib, however, was requested by military intelligence officers—one of whom told investigators that intimidating prisoners with unmuzzled dogs had been recommended by a two-star general.

The idea that the dog handlers were operating on their own did not seem plausible. Colonel Thomas Pappas, commander of the 205th Military Intelligence Brigade, said that when General Geoffrey Miller visited in the fall of 2003 he spoke admiringly of what could be accomplished with dogs. Said Pappas, "It was a technique I had personally discussed with General Miller when he was here. He said that they used military working dogs at Gitmo [Guantánamo] and that they were effective in setting the atmosphere for which, you know, you could get information."[72]

Miller, however, denied that he talked with Pappas about using guard dogs for interrogation or that dogs were used for interrogations at Guantánamo.

Regardless of who authorized the use of dogs, there is no doubt that the policy encouraged sadistic impulses by some. Specialist John Harold Ketzer, a military intelligence interrogator, testified that on January 13, 2004, he saw a dog team corner two male prisoners against a wall. One prisoner was hiding behind the other and screaming. "When I asked what was going on in the cell," Ketzer recalled, "the handler stated that he was just scaring them, and that he and another of the handlers was having a contest to see how many detainees they could get to urinate on themselves."[73]

"Ghosts" by the Dozens

There were other questionable practices that looked less like the whims of depraved soldiers and more like official policy that had gone terribly wrong. One such practice involved hiding prisoners' identities and whereabouts from the Red Cross—such prisoners are called "ghost detainees"[74] because no one knows their whereabouts. Hiding prisoners from the Red Cross is a violation of the Geneva Conventions since that organization's job is to monitor the treatment of all detainees. When governments secretly imprison people, prisoners can be abused without the Red Cross finding out. If the prisoner dies, the government can simply claim that it never saw the individual. Major General Taguba, who

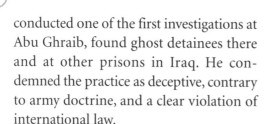

conducted one of the first investigations at Abu Ghraib, found ghost detainees there and at other prisons in Iraq. He condemned the practice as deceptive, contrary to army doctrine, and a clear violation of international law.

The International Committee of the Red Cross had suspected the United States was hiding detainees in prisons all over the world. One clue was that terror suspects reported as captured by the FBI did not turn up on prisoner lists. Meanwhile, the United States refused Red Cross demands to provide complete lists of the prisoners it was holding or to allow visits to all its prisons. Security concerns were usually given as the reason: The United States did not want terrorists to find out where or if their comrades were being held.

During the summer of 2004 the number of confirmed ghost detainees began climbing. Rumsfeld admitted in June that he had ordered a prisoner be hidden from the Red Cross. He said he did so at the request of the CIA. Although the prisoner had not been held at Abu Ghraib, the incident illustrated the involvement of high-level administration officials in prisoner handling. In the months following Rumsfeld's admission, the Defense Department conceded that it had found eight other hidden detainees.

Then, in September, General Paul Kern, who conducted an army investigation of the 205th Military Intelligence Brigade, told the Senate Armed Services Committee that the number of ghost detainees may have been as high as one hun-

dred. It was difficult to know the exact number because the CIA did not cooperate with the investigation. Critics of the theory that Abu Ghraib was caused by a few rogue soldiers note that moving ghost detainees from place to place underneath the noses of superiors was not something low-ranking soldiers could do. Higher-ranking officers must have been involved.

Suspicious Deaths

In addition to ghost detainess, the number of detainees that had died during their incarceration was suspiciously high. By the summer of 2004 at least thirty-seven prisoners had died while in U.S. custody. The fact that only two deaths could be connected to Abu Ghraib was particularly troubling because it suggested the problem went beyond just one prison. Of the thirty-seven confirmed deaths, at least ten were acknowledged as homicides by the Defense Department. Tellingly, all but one of the homicides occurred during or after an interrogation.

For example, after Major General Hamed Mowhoush, former chief of Iraqi air defenses, died in a detention facility north of Baghdad in 2003, the Defense Department released a statement reporting that he had died of natural causes—even though the autopsy report found that he had died from "asphyxia due to smothering and chest compression."[75] When the *Denver Post* investigated, they learned that two soldiers had wrapped the general tightly inside a sleeping bag and then sat

A photograph taken inside Abu Ghraib captures the isolation and anonymity of the detainees held there.

on his chest while covering his nose and mouth. Only after the Colorado paper published its charges did the Defense Department begin an investigation.

Degradation by Design?

Another indication that the abuse of prisoners at Abu Ghraib was not a lone occur-

rence was the character of the abuses. They systematically violated so many norms of Arab culture that it seemed unlikely to be a coincidence. For example, Gary Myers, a defense attorney for one of the MPs accused of the abuses, wondered whether a group of young reservists from rural Virginia could have come up with the idea that the best way

67

to embarrass Arabs and get them to talk was to have them walk around in the nude. A pamphlet given to Marine Corps troops being sent to Iraq, for example, clearly outlined behaviors that are offensive in Arab cultures. Among the "do's and don'ts" listed were these guidelines:

> Do not shame or humiliate a man in public. Shaming a man will cause him and his family to be anti-Coalition.
>
> Shame is given by placing hoods over a detainee's head. Avoid this practice.
>
> Placing a detainee on the ground or putting a foot on him implies you are God. This is one of the worst things we can do.
>
> The most important qualifier for all shame is a third party to witness the act. If you must do something likely to cause shame, remove the person from the view of others.[76]

Yet the guards' behavior at Abu Ghraib turned these guidelines upside down. Everything—especially the forced nudity, sexual games, and the public humiliation of groups of prisoners—seemed designed to produce the maximum humiliation. And the lack of effort to hide their activities led some observers to believe that the MPs thought they had the approval of their superiors. As Hersh put it, "The 372nds' [the 372nd Military Police company] abuse of prisoners seemed almost routine—a fact of Army life that the soldiers felt no need to hide."[77]

Official Findings: Confusion and Lack of Oversight

In late August the findings of two long-awaited investigations into the Abu Ghraib scandal were announced. As it turned out, neither report limited responsibility to a few rogue soldiers. However, although they did find ample evidence of poor leadership and unclear or conflicting goals, they did not find evidence of an official army policy that explicitly condoned torture.

The first report detailed an army investigation headed by Major General George Fay and two other generals. Fay's findings extended responsibility beyond the handful of military police and intelligence personnel previously implicated. The Fay report cited forty-four separate instances of abuses involving nearly fifty people. Although some observers considered the involvement of that many soldiers firm evidence of widespread mistreatment, others pointed out that in an army numbering tens of thousands, it was not that great a number.

Speaking with reporters at the Pentagon, General Paul J. Kern, one of the three generals heading the Fay report, seemed to agree with that viewpoint. "We found that the pictures you have seen, as revolting as they are, were not the result of any doctrine, training or policy failures, but violations of the law and misconduct. We've learned that there were leaders at Abu Ghraib who knew about this conduct, knew better, and did nothing. Some soldiers behaved improperly because they were confused by their experiences and direction."[78]

The other investigation, headed by former defense secretary James Schlesinger, found even more evidence of mistreatment. The Schlesinger panel received about three hundred reports of serious abuses and confirmed sixty-six of them before announcing their findings. Some of the brutality seems to have involved guards amusing themselves—those incidents could have been the work of just a few rogue soldiers. But at least a third of the confirmed abuses took place during interrogations. In those instances the guards were acting at the request of military intelligence officers, weakening the idea that the abuses were independent acts.

Both Schlesinger and Fay criticized the chaos caused by an unclear command structure. They particularly noted the confusion caused by differing interrogation policies. There were at least three separate interrogation policies in operation at Abu Ghraib—those cited in army field manuals, those used by interrogators who came

At a press conference, General Paul J. Kern explains the findings of the Fay report, which concluded that the abuse of prisoners was not the result of an official policy of torture.

Lieutenant General Ricardo S. Sanchez was criticized for frequently changing the rules for interrogations.

to Iraq from Afghanistan, and a third set modeled after techniques used at Guantánamo Bay. The situation was further complicated by the presence of CIA officers and civilians with unclear authority who nevertheless suggested ways to "soften up" detainees.

The Fay report concluded that the CIA's harsh detention and interrogation practices poisoned the atmosphere at Abu Ghraib. The CIA's abuse of prisoners encouraged military personnel to deviate from accepted practices. When MPs and military intelligence officers saw CIA officials mistreating prisoners with impunity, some began to do the same themselves. The report also described how the behavior spread. As the report stated, "What started as nakedness and humiliation, stress and physical training (exercise), carried over into sexual and physical assaults by a small group of morally corrupt and unsupervised soldiers and civilians."[79] The report also criticized the CIA for not cooperating with investigators. Because the CIA denied access to its documents and personnel, a full accounting of what really happened at Abu Ghraib may never be made.

Higher-Ups Faulted

But sections of the report not released publicly (but dug up by the *New York Times*) were critical of the top commander in Iraq, General Ricardo S. Sanchez. In the fall of 2003 Sanchez changed the rules for interrogations three times in thirty days. The resulting confusion contributed to numerous violations of the Geneva Conventions. Another part of the report found that harsh practices previously used in questioning al Qaeda and Taliban detainees in Afghanistan and Guantánamo were unlawfully transferred to Iraq.

In assessing responsibility for Abu Ghraib, the Schlesinger panel pointed further up the chain of command. It chastised the Defense Department's most senior civilian and military leaders for setting the stage for abuses. They were accused of issuing unclear orders, planning poorly, and responding slowly to reports of problems.

Testimony by the officer who oversaw interrogations at Abu Ghraib also suggested that senior officials shared some of the blame. According to Lieutenant Colonel Steven Jordan, officials in Washington were intensely interested in the interrogations at Abu Ghraib. Jordan claimed that his boss, Colonel Thomas Pappas, told him more than once that their intelligence reports were being read by Defense Secretary Rumsfeld and by officials at CIA headquarters. Jordan's word may not be completely trustworthy—General Taguba believed that Jordan had lied to his investigators on several occasions. Still, the main

thrust of Jordan's statement matches recollections of other officers who reported intense interest from higher-ups.

Although the Schlesinger panel did not mention Rumsfeld by name, it implies that he bore considerable responsibility—for not providing enough troops and for not clarifying policies. It noted that when General Karpinski asked for more troops to help her overstretched forces at Abu Ghraib, that request was denied. Instead, she was told to "wear her stars"[80] (that is, act like a general) and solve the problem by herself. Both the Fay and Schlesinger reports strongly suggest that the problems at Abu Ghraib were the result of leadership failures and a policy spinning out of control.

"A Simple Truth"

Although neither report said so specifically, both supported the conclusion reached by award-winning reporter, Mark Danner. A staff writer for the *New Yorker* and professor of journalism at the University of California at Berkeley, Danner wrote:

> Behind the exotic brutality so painstakingly recorded at Abu Ghraib, and the multiple tangled plotlines that will be teased out in the coming weeks and months . . . lies a simple truth, well known but not yet publicly admitted in Washington: that since the attacks of September 11, 2001, officials of the United States at various locations around the world, from Bagram in Afghanistan to Guantánamo in Cuba

to Abu Ghraib in Iraq, have been torturing prisoners.[81]

After September 11, the military's longtime commitment to the Geneva Conventions eroded under an aggressive plan to deal with terrorism. Harsh interrogation techniques used by the CIA in Afghanistan began to be used by the military as well— first at Guantánamo Bay and then in Iraq.

An Iraqi prisoner peers through the bars of his cell at the Al-Ma'qal prison in Basra. The Geneva Conventions were designed to protect his right to humane treatment.

Pressure to do something about a rising insurgency led to the same tactics being used against Iraqi citizens without connections to terrorism. An article in *USA Today* may best sum up the scandal's causes: "There's no evidence of a high-level order to engage broadly in torture. Just the opposite. But neither can the problem be blamed on a few bad actors. At the very least, it suggests indifference and conflicting goals at the highest levels that encouraged the abusers."[82]

Of the hundreds of thousands of American soldiers who served in Iraq, only a relative handful abused Iraqi prisoners. Although those who did so were held accountable, both senior military and civilian leaders share blame for failing to set clear guidelines on how prisoners should be treated.

Chapter Five

The Legacy of Abu Ghraib

The costs and effects of Abu Ghraib are substantial—and yet to be fully determined. When legal proceedings against the scandal's most visible participants began, it seemed likely that the scandal's ultimate cost would hinge on whether the U.S. government was seen as making a sincere effort to find and punish all those responsible. Despite unanswered questions about the ultimate responsibility, it is likely that the scandal had tarnished America's image as a defender of human rights and limited its international influence. The images of Abu Ghraib became recruiting tools for terrorists and increased the odds that American soldiers captured in future conflicts would be mistreated. The scandal also led to restrictions on presidential powers and raised questions about America's moral authority in the war on terrorism.

When the first photographs of U.S. soldiers humiliating and torturing prisoners at Abu Ghraib were released, there was a sense that the way the situation was handled might mitigate the damage. Many Americans pointed out that, as appalling as the pictures were, the responsible parties would be found and justice would be served. Secretary of State Colin Powell sought to reassure foreign leaders that the situation would be corrected. "Watch America," he said. "Watch how we deal with this. Watch how America will do the right thing."[83]

Changes Caused by Abu Ghraib

Both the judicial system and the Bush administration made immediate attempts to rectify what happened at Abu Ghraib.

On June 23, 2004, in what was seen by many as an attempt to undo the damage done by the "torture memos," the Justice Department announced that it was rewriting its legal advice on how interrogations could be conducted. A few days later the CIA said that it was suspending the use of interrogation techniques at its detention facilities around the world until a ruling could be made on what was permissible. Suspended techniques included suffocating prisoners until they were close to losing consciousness, shining bright lights in their eyes, blasting them with loud noises, and forcing them into stressful positions.

Also in June, the Senate passed a measure attempting to limit U.S. interrogation techniques to those that the U.S. would consider

Iraqi citizens demonstrate in Baghdad in May 2004, as the first American soldiers accused of abusing prisoners are arraigned in court.

Finding Out Who Knew

Elizabeth Holtzman is a former congress-woman from New York who served on the House Judiciary Committee during the impeachment of Richard Nixon. In an article for Newsday, *she voiced the belief, shared by many, that undoing the damage of Abu Ghraib required a full accounting of the role of higher ranking officials:*

"We need to know what directives [President] Bush gave for CIA and military interrogations in Iraq. We also need to know what the president and his subordinates, such as Secretary of Defense Donald Rumsfeld, knew about inhuman treatments of Iraqi prisoners—and when they knew it and what they did about it. . . .

We know that the orders for inhuman treatment came directly from Lt. Gen. Ricardo Sanchez, the top military officer in Iraq. But we don't yet know where he got his orders. . . .

We simply cannot prosecute only the 'small fry' [that is, the lone soldier] for this scandal that has undercut our mission in Iraq and besmirched our reputation. We have to demonstrate the rule of law applies to everyone responsible, including the president, if the evidence warrants. . . . There must be a thorough investigation of the higher-ups, and that requires a full congressional inquiry and the appointment of a special prosecutor.

The horrendous mistreatment of Iraqi prisoners has disgraced the United States and endangered our troops and citizens. The best way to vindicate our country and undo the damage done to Iraqi prisoners is to ensure that everyone responsible is held accountable—without exceptions. We may pay a terrible price if we fail to do so."

legal for other nations to use. The proposed law also urged that detainees be released or prosecuted promptly—not held indefinitely.

In July 2004 the Supreme Court ruled that the president could not lock up suspected terrorists indefinitely without first giving them a chance to show that they had been wrongfully captured. Abu Ghraib was not mentioned in the decision, but according to Steven Shapiro, national legal director for the American Civil Liberties Union, "it is hard to believe that it did not affect the court and reinforce the view that unchecked power invites abuse."[84]

In the immediate aftermath of Abu Ghraib, charges were filed against six of the low-ranking soldiers whose faces could be identified from the photographs. The Defense Department was not disposed to act kindly toward these men and women. One official at the Pentagon referred to them as "the six morons who lost the war."[85] Because twenty-four-year-old Specialist Jeremy Sivits agreed to plead guilty to all the criminal charges filed against him, he was the first accused offender to be sentenced. Sivits was given a year in prison and a discharge for bad conduct. He described the situation at Abu Ghraib as something out of a horror movie and apologized for what he had done. "It was wrong. It should not have happened," he testified. "I've let everybody down."[86] In October 2004, Staff Sgt. Ivan "Chip" Frederick followed Sivits to prison. Frederick was given a sentence of eight years.

Sivits and Frederick were two of the seven low-ranking reservists initially accused of crimes. They and their fellow military policemen and policewomen all defended their actions in a similar fashion. Private First Class Lyndie England, a female soldier seen in photos leading a naked Iraqi around on a dog leash, said she had acted at the request of intelligence officers who wanted her to soften up prisoners for questioning. Sergeant Javal S. Davis, another of the military policemen charged with crimes, was asked why he did not report the abusive behavior he saw. He replied that Military Intelligence controlled that wing of the prison and that he and the other military police assumed that if they were doing anything wrong, someone would have said something. Davis was asked about Specialist Charles Graner, who seemed to have been involved in some of the most brutal abuses:

> The MI [military intelligence] staffs, to my understanding, have been giving Graner compliments on the way he has been handling the MI holds [prisoners held by military intelligence], [an] example being statements like "Good job, they're breaking down

real fast"; "They answer every question"; "They're giving out good information, finally"; and "Keep up the good work"—stuff like that.[87]

Like many of the MPs charged with offenses, Sivits pointed out that he and other prison guards had been working alongside military intelligence personnel who encouraged the very behavior he and others were now being punished for. Not until September 2004, however, was the first military intelligence soldier court-martialed. Specialist Armin Cruz was sentenced to eight months in jail for mistreating prisoners. In January 2005, Graner was sentenced to ten years in jail for his role in the abuse.

Did More Deserve Justice?

Although dozens of other MPs and intelligence specialists were facing punishment, some human rights advocates and other observers began to complain the investigators were focused too intently on the low end of the chain of command. It was believed that higher-ranking officials might be responsible for pieces of the puzzle but were not being investigated. It was still unclear, for example, who had ordered General Geoffrey Miller, the former commander at Guantánamo, to overhaul interrogation practices at Abu Ghraib. It was also unclear what intelligence recommendations Miller had made—and which ones were then approved by General Ricardo Sanchez, the top commander in Iraq. Sanchez told Congress he never approved the illegal use of

Just Following Orders

Most of the MPs accused of abusing Iraqis inside Abu Ghraib said that they were following orders given to them by intelligence officers. The "following orders" defense is also called the Nuremberg defense because it was used in the Nuremberg trials which prosecuted Nazi war criminals after World War II.

Germans accused of war crimes claimed they were not responsible for their actions because they were only doing what their superiors told them. That was not considered a sufficient excuse—the judges at Nuremberg said that the accused should have known the orders were criminal. Likewise, during the Vietnam War, an American officer named William Calley used a similar defense unsuccessfully. Calley and his men killed most of the people living in a village called My Lai.

Lawyers for the accused MPs at Abu Ghraib, however, note that there is a big difference between murder and abuse. They also question whether reservists knew enough about the Geneva Conventions to disobey orders that violated them. "Ask any American what the Geneva Conventions require in the gray area of intimidation, or ask a young, unsophisticated private guarding a prison while their buddies on the outside are being shot," said one defense lawyer. "You're going to do exactly as they did if told to."

Although a jury could conclude that an accused soldier might not have known he or she was breaking the law, the accused faced a huge problem with such a defense—they also had to prove who gave them the orders. However, many of the officers and civilians working at Abu Ghraib never clearly identified themselves. In addition, some of the superior officers who were there denied giving orders to torture prisoners.

dogs, yet he was not asked why his signature appeared on orders allowing interrogators to use dogs and other illegal measures. Perhaps the most important question that was left unanswered was the matter of exactly who, if anyone, in the Pentagon knew of the interrogation practices going on at Abu Ghraib.

The Defense Department launched at least eight separate investigations after Abu Ghraib hit the news. Yet, the independence of the investigators—all of whom were working for their ultimate boss, Secretary Rumsfeld—was questioned from the very beginning. "How," asked Reed Brody, special counsel for Human Rights Watch, "are investigators appointed by Rumsfeld going to determine whether Rumsfeld ordered, condoned, or acquiesced in torture?"[88] Brody cited the first investigation conducted by Lieutenant General Paul Mikolashek, the army's inspector general. Mikolashek looked at ninety-four cases of detainee abuse in Afghanistan and Iraq. Brody believed that this many cases of abuse were clear evidence of a widespread pattern of abuse that must have been either condoned or ignored by superior officers. But Mikolashek concluded that the abuses did not result from any policy and were not the fault of senior officials. Instead, he said, they were unauthorized actions taken by a few individuals.

General Karpinski, who was relieved of her command, was the highest-ranking officer to be punished for Abu Ghraib. In public statements she insisted that she was being made a scapegoat for others above her who were more responsible. She claims that she argued with Miller when he recommended turning over the prison to military intelligence but that he insisted that she do so because his recommendation had the backing of Sanchez. Speaking of the

General Janis Karpinski was in charge of Iraqi prisons during the Abu Ghraib abuses. She is the highest-ranking official to be punished for the scandal thus far.

area where the worst abuses occurred, she said, "That particular cellblock was under the control of the military intelligence command at the time and in fact from November on Abu Ghraib Prison was under the control of the military intelligence command."[89] Karpinski's attorney, Neal Puckett, claims that the Taguba investigation's mission was limited to finding out what was wrong with the 800th MP Brigade and therefore was not likely to find wrongdoing elsewhere. He accused the investigation of not being interested in finding the truth: "The direction was not something terrible has happened, go find out what went wrong and . . . then we'll deal with it."[90]

Abu Ghraib and Arab Anger

Whether all of the appropriate people were brought to justice in America mattered little to the average Iraqi. The pictures of beatings and humiliations of their fellow citizens hardened Iraqi attitudes toward the coalition. Even before the abuses were revealed, many had been enraged by the treatment being doled out at Abu Ghraib and other prisons. Abdullah Abdurazzaq, a detainee who was mistreated at Abu Ghraib and then later released because he was innocent is still angry about what happened to him. "How can we not hate the Americans after the treatment we have received?" he asks. "It is not human."[91]

Inadequate record keeping by American soldiers who did not speak Arabic in-

creased the problems at Iraq's prisons and also hardened attitudes. Thousands of Iraqis were unable to find out where, or even if, missing family members were imprisoned. Misspelled names or data-entry errors made it impossible to locate hundreds of detainees. Sometimes detainee numbers were not on file or linked to a different name. Once behind bars, many detainees, including some children, were kept there indefinitely—even those who had done nothing wrong. Coalition leaders admitted that many detainees were imprisoned unnecesarily. All these indignities and humiliations contributed to a mounting frustration.

In a television interview about Abu Ghraib and its aftermath, Hisham Melhem, a correspondent for the Lebanese newspaper, *As-Safir*, described how the situation had affected Arab attitudes about the United States: "If you wanted to write a script or a scenario as to how you undermine the credibility of the United States in the Middle East today, you couldn't have done a better job. . . . I think one could argue if you have any illusions about winning hearts and minds in Iraq and the Arab world for that matter, you should forget that."[92]

However, some Americans believed that Arab outrage was extremely hypocritical given the lack of concern for human rights in the Arab world. "Indeed," wrote Frida Ghitis in the *St. Louis Post-Dispatch*, "some of those expressing shock and horror at the very thought of prisoner mistreatment are governments whose use of

An Iraqi insurgent fires a mortar round at coalition forces. Attacks on coalition forces in Iraq more than doubled after news of Abu Ghraib became public.

torture is routine."[93] Whether or not the outrage was hypocritical, it was definitely widespread within Iraq itself. *Newsweek* reported that the first poll taken inside Iraq after Abu Ghraib showed that the scandal had accelerated a long-term decline in support for the U.S. occupation. Although 71 percent of Iraqis said the incidents at Abu Ghraib surprised them, most agreed that such abuses were widespread. And, a distressingly high number—54 percent—said they believed that "all Americans behave this way."[94]

Increased Violence

The Iraqi loss of confidence in the American mission in Iraq went hand in hand with greater support for the resistance and increased violence. Although a direct cause and effect relation was impossible to prove, the Abu Ghraib scandal seemed to have provoked the insurgency and significantly endangered coalition troops. As one Iraqi, Majid al-Salim, put it, "Americans are driving people into the arms of the Maqawama [the resistance]. We now look back at Saddam's era with nostalgia. He was a good leader. There was security."[95]

In the months after the scandal broke, the level of violence and bloodshed inside Iraq climbed steeply. Attacks on U.S. and other occupying forces increased to between forty and fifty a day (more than double what they had been early in the year) and continued to rise. In September 2004 there were more than twenty-three hundred attacks on civilian and military targets inside Iraq.

American soldiers who had never abused any detainees were angered that what had happened at Abu Ghraib made their jobs more dangerous. Mike Billips, a reporter for *Time,* visited soldiers near the Fort Stewart army base in Hinesville, Georgia, not long after the Abu Ghraib scandal broke. The soldiers he talked to were either on their way to Iraq or had just returned. None were pleased about what had happened.

"It makes me mad that we fight this war to help these folks and somebody does this [that is, abuse prisoners],"[96] said Chris Crozier, a mechanic with the 3rd Infantry Division. Billips found that while the soldiers might disagree on who was responsible, all agreed that the soldiers on the ground would have to face the rage that abuse had sparked. The rising death toll of Americans since the scandal suggests that the soldiers' fears were justified.

Another long-term effect of Abu Ghraib could be that American soldiers captured in future conflicts will face mistreatment. According to journalist Seymour Hersh, a two-star general complained to him about what he felt was a likely outcome of the Abu Ghraib prisoner abuse scandal. "Look, I take my boys into combat, and the last thing that I want is to know that [if] my boys get captured, they're going to be stripped naked, hands tied and hoods put over their heads. . . . We've opened the door for them to do it to us more."[97]

Soldiers were not the only Americans who had to pay a price for what happened inside Abu Ghraib. Businessmen, travelers, and diplomats all faced increased danger as a rash of kidnappings and beheadings swept the country. In May 2004 a U.S. businessman named Nick Berg was captured inside Iraq by Islamic militants. A grisly videotape of him being beheaded was then sent to news organizations. Berg's killers claimed that his murder was carried out to avenge the abuses of Iraqis in Abu Ghraib. Likewise in June, when Islamic radicals in Saudi Arabia kidnapped a U.S. military contractor in Riyadh, they announced that they had a legal right to treat him the same way that Iraqi prisoners had been treated at Abu Ghraib.

An Overblown Scandal?

Despite the surge in violence, many Americans believed that the scandal and its fallout were greatly exaggerated. Although the abuse of prisoners was abhorrent, they argued that America on the whole treats its prisoners far better than most other countries. Some suspected that the uproar over Abu Ghraib was being manipulated for political gain by forces opposed to the Bush administration. Senator James Inhofe of Oklahoma expressed that viewpoint when he spoke out during congressional hearings on the matter. "I'm probably not the only one up at this table that is more outraged by the outrage than we are by the treatment," he said. "I have to say ... that I would guess that these prisoners wake up every morning thanking Allah that Saddam Hussein is not in charge of these prisons."[98]

Others pointed to the way the scandal was being handled as proof that the United States was acting honorably. "In all the furor over the photographs from Abu Ghraib,

A lone soldier walks along a corridor at Abu Ghraib. Some Americans believe the abuse was justified as a means of obtaining information from suspected terrorists.

what's been overlooked by many is the fact that the American military was not only already investigating allegations but announced that the inquiry had begun three months ago," wrote Mortimer B. Zuckerman in *U.S. News & World Report.* "Major General Antonio Taguba's investigation was thorough and his conclusion was that the abuse was the result of the actions of a handful of guards and their superiors, not the result of an official policy or order."[99]

Americans like Gordon Bishop, an author, historian, and syndicated newspaper columnist, were similarly disappointed in the uproar over Abu Ghraib:

> Why are American leaders apologizing for fighting terrorists? . . . There never should be apologies in a global war on terrorists. . . . What happened at a prison in Iraq to some prisoners of war has been blown all out of proportion by the self-righteous, politically correct liberals opposing the "War on Terror." President Bush and Defense Secretary Donald Rumsfeld did not have to apologize for the humiliation suffered by some Iraqi prisoners at the hands of a few dumb soldiers.[100]

Bishop believed that any comparison between U.S. military treatment of prisoners at Abu Ghraib and Saddam's famed brutalities was innaccurate and ridiculous.

Still other Americans believed the nation was in a struggle to the death with Islamic terrorists and thus applauded any action that helped defend the country, including the rough treatment of terrorists. Writer Tammy

Bruce vividly expresses that viewpoint in an article for *FrontPageMagazine.com.*

> I believe when it comes to Al-Qaida leadership and operatives, anything goes. I don't care if you put women's underwear on their heads, or frankly, even pull out a few fingernails of those responsible for mass murder, to unmask their continuing plans for the genocide of civilized peoples. . . . It's called "torture lite," it works, and I'm all for whatever it takes to get information, and, yes, to punish and annihilate terrorist leadership around the world.[101]

Abu Ghraib and the War on Terrorism

However, one of the more troubling aspects of Abu Ghraib is that it has the potential to make the apprehension of terrorists more difficult. In order to win the war on terrorism the United States will need the cooperation of nations where terrorists seek refuge. But the prison scandal helped spur a sharp rise in anti-Americanism all over the Middle East and, to a lesser extent, Islamic nations elsewhere. In that atmosphere, cooperation may be difficult.

The photographs from Abu Ghraib inflamed public opinion. Honor is extremely important in Arab culture and the images from inside the prison seem to show the human dignity of Arabs under systematic attack. Newspapers and television stations in the Arab world ran many more pictures of Abu Ghraib than did the Western me-

Did Abu Ghraib Help the Terrorists?

Reed Brody, a counsel for Human Rights Watch and author of Disappeared: The U.S. Ghost Detainees, *makes the case that the rough treatment of terrorist suspects at Abu Ghraib and elsewhere weakened the war on terror and lessened respect for the United States. In an article for the* International Herald Tribune, *he explains why:*

"These [the detainees] are not nice men, to say the least. Why should we care about what happens to them? First, because, despite the information apparently gleaned from some of these suspects, overall the U.S. treatment of its prisoners has been a boon rather than a setback for Al Qaeda, and has thereby made the world less safe from terror. As the Sept. 11 commission [the panel that studied the attacks of September 11 and made recommendations on how to deal with terrorism] said, 'allegations that the United States abused prisoners in its custody make it harder to build the diplomatic, political, and military alliances the government will need.'

Second, the torture and 'disappearance' of prisoners by the United States invites all the unsavory governments in the world to do the same. Indeed, countries from Sudan to Zimbabwe have already cited Abu Ghraib and other U.S. actions to justify their own practices or to blunt criticism.

But our concern must stem, first and foremost, from the acceptance of methods which are antithetical to a democracy and which betray the U.S. identity as a nation of law. If the United States embraces the torture and 'disappearance' of its opponents, it abandons its ideals and becomes a lesser nation."

---

dia. They were also much more likely to interpret the abuses as a direct affront to their culture and religion. A claim heard often in Iraq was that America was just like Saddam's ruling party—a regime that tortured and killed thousands of devout Muslims.

Meanwhile, extremist Islamic groups were all too happy to encourage that kind of thinking because it made people more receptive to their anti-American messages. The pictures from Abu Ghraib served their purposes well. The Islamic religion teaches that it is shameful and immoral to expose one's body in public and has strict rules regarding sexual behavior. Religious Muslims were outraged to see the near-pornographic pictures of fellow Muslims being shamed in such a way. It was all the proof that some devout Muslims needed that the United States was indeed a godless and profane country that must be driven from the Middle East, as the extremist groups claimed.

Indeed, some argue that after the prison scandal, attitudes toward the United States in the Middle East had reached an all-time low. Stephen Holmes, research director of the Center for Law and Security at New York University, believes that Arabs and Muslims who were once friendly or neutral toward the United States are becoming increasingly

The Abu Ghraib abuse photos have angered many in the Arab world. Here, Iranian protestors burn the American flag in front of the U.S. embassy in Tehran.

hostile. "This," he says, "is a very dangerous development, since it means that anti-American attitudes are putting more Middle Easterners beyond the reach of diplomacy."[102]

On the other hand, others were convinced that the disturbing images from Abu Ghraib would have no effect on the larger war on terror. According to author Gordon Cucullu, worrying about public opinion in the Middle East is pointless:

> From a practical standpoint, it is difficult to see *how* [they could hate us more].... They danced in the street in joy [on September 11, 2001]. They bounce on the hoods of destroyed Humvees and drag American bodies through the streets....
>
> I worry less about the Arab Street [Arab public opinion] losing its "good will" than I would fret about a recurring Ice Age.[103]

Questioning What America Stands For

It is likely, however, that the legacy of the Abu Ghraib scandal will have far-reaching consequences for the military and for America's moral authority in the world. Until September 11, 2001, soldiers were bound by a strict code as to how to treat prisoners. In essence, the policy was that the United States treated prisoners as it wanted its own soldiers to be treated if captured. That code of honor appears to have eroded at Abu Ghraib and elsewhere.

Fiaz Khan, a citizen of Pakistan, outlines the challenge facing the nation in the aftermath of Abu Ghraib. "People look up to the ideals of the American constitution and recognize it as America's real glory and greatness," says Khan. "Abu Ghraib . . . [makes] it difficult to distinguish the U.S. government from its enemies."[104]

Whether the damage will be long lasting remains to be seen. If the affair is handled in a way that seems just to fair-minded people—and more abuses do not surface in the meantime—then the cost in American influence and prestige may be contained. President Bush and many others have called the war on terrorism a war of ideas. "Now, as the photographs of Abu Ghraib make clear," says Mark Danner, "it has also become a struggle over what, if anything, really does represent America."[105]

Notes

Introduction: A Dark Day in America

1. Quoted in Marian Wilkinson, "Generals in a Labyrinth of Blame," *The Age*, May 15, 2004. www.theage.com.
2. Quoted in *Washington Post*, "The Homicide Cases," May 28, 2004, p. A22.
3. Andy Rooney, "Our Darkest Days Are Here," *CBSNEWS.com*, May 23, 2004. www.cbsnews.com.
4. Quoted in Nicholas Blanford, "To Arabs, Photos Confirm Brutal U.S.," *Christian Science Monitor*, May 3, 2004. www.csmonitor.com.
5. Quoted in Nicholas Blanford, "Iraqi Artists Depict Anger over Abu Graib," *Christian Science Monitor*, June 15, 2004. www.csmonitor.com.

Chapter One: Iraq and the War on Terror

6. Quoted in T.D. Allman, *Rogue State: America at War with the World*. New York: Nation, 2004, p. 215.
7. Quoted in Allman, *Rogue State*, p. 215.
8. Quoted in John Newhouse, *Imperial America: The Bush Assault on the World Order*. New York: Knopf, 2003, p. 12.
9. George W. Bush, remarks on Iraq at Cincinnati Museum Center, Cincinnati, Ohio, October 7, 2002. www.whitehouse.gov.
10. Quoted in *CBSNEWS.com*, "Abuse of Iraqi POWs by GIs Probed," April 28, 2004. www.cbsnews.com.
11. Quoted in Douglas Jehl and Kate Zernike, "Scant Evidence Cited in Long Detention of Iraqis," *New York Times*, May 30, 2004. www.nytimes.com.
12. Quoted in Seymour Hersh, "The Gray Zone," *New Yorker*, May 24, 2004. www.newyorker.com.
13. Quoted in John Barry, Mark Hosenball, and Babak Dehghanpisheh, "Abu Ghraib and Beyond," *Newsweek*, May 17, 2004, p. 28.
14. Quoted in Barry, Hosenball, and Dehghanpisheh, "Abu Ghraib and Beyond," p. 28.
15. Quoted in Nat Parry, "Bush's Apex of Unlimited Power," *Consortium News*, June 15, 2004. www.consortiumnews.com.

Chapter Two: Tales of Torture

16. Quoted in Toni Locy, "Interrogators Hid Identities," *USA Today*, May 27, 2004. www.usatoday.com.
17. Quoted in Hersh, "The Gray Zone."
18. Quoted in Seymour Hersh, "Torture at Abu Ghraib," *New Yorker*, May 10, 2004, p. 44.
19. Quoted in Hersh, "Torture at Abu Ghraib," p. 45.
20. Quoted in William Saletan, "Rape Rooms: A Chronology," *Slate*, May 5, 2004. http://slate.msn.com.
21. Quoted in Hersh, "Torture at Abu Ghraib," p. 43.

22. *WashingtonPost.com*, "Sworn Statements by Abu Ghraib Detainees," www.washingtonpost.com.

23. Quoted in Scott Higham and Joe Stephens, "New Details of Prison Abuse Emerge," *Washington Post*, May 21, 2004, p. A01.

24. Quoted in Higham and Stephens, "New Details of Prison Abuse Emerge," p. A01.

25. Quoted in Dahr Jamail, "The Student Is Gone; the Master Has Arrived," *New Standard*, June 13, 2004. http://blog.new standardnews.net.

26. Quoted in Higham and Stephens, "New Details of Prison Abuse Emerge," p. A01.

27. *WashingtonPost.com*, "Sworn Statements by Abu Ghraib Detainees."

28. *WashingtonPost.com*, "Sworn Statements by Abu Ghraib Detainees."

29. Quoted in Seymour Hersh, "Chain of Command," *New Yorker*, May 17, 2004. www.newyorker.com.

30. Quoted in *WashingtonPost.com*, "Sworn Statements by Abu Ghraib Detainees."

Chapter Three: A Scandal Breaks

31. Robert Collier, "Iraqi Detainees Report 'Inhumane Treatment,'" *San Francisco Chronicle, SFGate.com*, July 29, 2003. www.sfgate.com.

32. Quoted in Mark Danner, "The Logic of Torture," *New York Review of Books*, June 24, 2004.

33. Quoted in Douglas Jehl and Neil A. Lewis, "Army: Some Iraqis Exempt from Geneva," *San Diego Union-Tribune, New York Times* News Services, May 23, 2004. www.signonsandiego.com.

34. Quoted in Luke Harding, "Torture Commonplace, Say Inmates' Families," *The Guardian*, May 3, 2004. www.guardian.co.uk.

35. Quoted in Hersh, "Torture at Abu Ghraib," p. 45.

36. Quoted in Hersh, "Torture at Abu Ghraib," p. 44.

37. Quoted in Hersh, "Torture at Abu Ghraib," p. 44.

38. *StarNewsOnline.com*, "Unit Says It Gave Earlier Warning of Abuse," June 17, 2004. www.wilmingtonstar.com.

39. *StarNewsOnline.com*, "Unit Says It Gave Earlier Warning of Abuse."

40. Quoted in *CNN.com*, "Army Report Documents Mistreatment of Iraqi Prisoners," May 4, 2004. http://edition.cnn.com.

41. Quoted in Hersh, "Torture at Abu Ghraib," p. 44.

42. Quoted in Hersh, "Chain of Command."

43. George W. Bush, remarks on efforts to globally promote women's human rights, White House, March 12, 2004. www.whitehouse.gov.

44. Quoted in *CBSNEWS.com*, "Abuse of Iraqi POWs by GIs Probed."

45. Quoted in *CBSNEWS.com*, "Abuse of Iraqi POWs by GIs Probed."

46. *WorldPress.org*, "Iraqi Prisoner Abuse Draws International Media Outrage," May 12, 2004. www.worldpress.org.

47. *WorldPress.org*, "Iraqi Prisoner Abuse Draws International Media Outrage."

48. Quoted in Eric Roston and J.F.O. McAllister, "Humiliation in an Iraqi Jail," *Time*, May 10, 2004, p. 20.

49. PBS, "Prisoner Abuse Fallout," transcript,

Online News Hour, May 4, 2004. www.pbs.org.

50. *Al-Ahram Weekly On-Line,* "MPs Slam Abu Ghraib Scandal," May 13–19, 2004. http://weekly.ahram.org.

51. Quoted in Mike Allen and Susan Schmidt, "Memo on Interrogation Tactics Is Disavowed," *Washington Post,* June 23, 2004, p. A01.

52. Ross Edwards, letter to *Time* (Canada), June 7, 2004, p. 2.

53. Chase Hoozer, letter to *Time* (Canada), June 7, 2004, p. 2.

54. Quoted in *CBSNEWS.com,* "Rush: MPs Just Blowing Off Steam," May 14, 2004. www.cbsnews.com.

55. Quoted in Johanna McGeary, "The Scandal's Growing Stain," *Time,* May 17, 2004, p. 26.

56. Quoted in Evan Thomas, "No Good Defense," *Newsweek,* May 17, 2004, p. 30.

57. George W. Bush, interview by Al Arabiya Television, White House, March 12, 2004. www.whitehouse.gov.

58. *Washington Post,* "The Homicide Cases."

Chapter Four: Bad Apples—or Bad Policy?

59. Quoted in John Barry, Michael Hirsh, and Michael Isikoff, "The Roots of Torture," *Newsweek,* May 24, 2004, p. 27.

60. Quoted in Barry, Hosenball, and Dehghanpisheh, "Abu Ghraib and Beyond."

61. Quoted in McGeary, "The Scandal's Growing Stain."

62. Quoted in *CBSNEWS.com,* "Abuse of Iraqi POWs by GIs Probed."

63. Quoted in *St. Louis Post-Dispatch,*

"Prison Abuse: Passing the Buck," August 8, 2004. www.stltoday.com.

64. *St. Petersburg Times Online,* "The Torture Memos," June 13, 2004. www.sptimes.com.

65. Quoted in Neil A. Lewis and Eric Schmitt, "Lawyers Decided Bans on Torture Didn't Bind Bush," *New York Times,* June 8, 2004, p. A1.

66. Quoted in R. Jeffrey Smith, "Lawyer for State Dept. Disputed Detainee Memo," *Washington Post,* June 24, 2004, p. A07.

67. Quoted in Dana Priest and R. Jeffrey Smith, "Memo Offered Justification for Use of Torture," *Washington Post,* June 8, 2004, p. A01.

68. Quoted in John Diamond, "Rumsfeld OK'd Harsh Treatment," *USA Today,* June 23, 2004. www.usatoday.com.

69. Quoted in Dana Priest and Barton Gellman, "US Decries Abuse but Defends Interrogations," *Washington Post,* December 26, 2002, p. A01.

70. Quoted in Priest and Gellman, "US Decries Abuse but Defends Interrogations."

71. Quoted in Priest and Gellman, "US Decries Abuse but Defends Interrogations."

72. Quoted in R. Jeffrey Smith, "General Is Said to Have Urged Use of Dogs," *Washington Post,* May 26, 2004, p. A01.

73. Quoted in Josh White and Scott Higham, "Use of Dogs to Scare Prisoners Was Authorized," *Washington Post,* June 11, 2004, p. A01.

74. *ABCNews.com,* "Lawmakers Troubled by 'Ghost Detainees,'" September 10, 2004. http://abcnews.go.com.

75. *Washington Post,* "The Homicide Cases."

76. Quoted in Danner, "The Logic of Torture."

77. Hersh, "Torture at Abu Ghraib," pp. 43–44.

78. Quoted in Josh White, "Abuse Report Widens Scope of Culpability," *Washington Post,* August 26, 2004. www.washingtonpost.com.

79. Quoted in Thomas E. Ricks, "Incidents Grew in Severity, Report Says," *Washington Post,* August 26, 2004, p. A17.

80. Quoted in Mark Thompson and Elaine Shannon, "The Verdict on Rumsfeld," *Time,* September 6, 2004, p. 16.

81. Danner, "The Logic of Torture."

82. *USA Today,* "How Innocent Iraqis Came to Be Abused as Terrorists," June 10, 2004, p. 14A.

Chapter Five: The Legacy of Abu Ghraib

83. Quoted in Reed Brody, "Where's the Promised Accountability for U.S. Abuse of Prisoners in Iraq?" *St. Paul Pioneer Press,* August 5, 2004, p. 12A.

84. Joan Biskupic, "High Court Protected Liberties by Limiting Presidential Power," *USA Today,* July 2, 2004, p. 4A.

85. Quoted in Tom Regan, "Six Morons Who Lost the War," *Christian Science Monitor,* May 4, 2004. www.csmonitor.com.

86. Quoted in *CNN.com,* "Soldier Sentenced to 1 Year in Iraqi Prisoner Abuse." www.cnn.com.

87. Quoted in Danner, "The Logic of Torture."

88. Brody, "Where's the Promised Accountability for U.S. Abuse of Prisoners in Iraq?"

89. Janis Karpinski, interview on *American Morning,* Interview on transcript, CNN, May 4, 2004. http:// transcripts.cn.com.

90. Quoted in Karpinski, interview.

91. Quoted in Scott Wilson, "Angry Ex-Detainees Tell of Abuse," *Washington Post,* May 3, 2004, p. A01.

92. Quoted in PBS, "Prisoner Abuse Fallout."

93. Frida Ghitis, "People Who Live in Glass Houses," *St. Louis Post-Dispatch,* May 10, 2004, p. B7.

94. Quoted in Michael Hirsh, "Grim Numbers," *Newsweek,* June 16, 2004. http://msnbc.msn.com.

95. Quoted in Harding, "Torture Commonplace, Say Inmates' Families."

96. Quoted in Mike Billips, "Confronting a Scandal's Debris," *Time,* May 24, 2004, p. 50.

97. Quoted in Seymour Hersh, interview with John Weisman, *Military.com,* June 1, 2004. www.military.com.

98. Quoted in *CBSNEWS.com,* "GOP Sen.: 'Outraged at Outrage,'" May 11, 2004. www.cbsnews.com.

99. Mortimer B. Zuckerman, "A Bit of Perspective, Please," *U.S. News & World Report,* May 24, 2004. www.usnews.com.

100. Gordon Bishop, "America Owes No Apologies for Fighting Terrorists," *American Daily,* May 21, 2004. www.americandaily.com/article/112.

101. Tammy Bruce, "Why Abu Ghraib Matters," *FrontPageMagazine.com,* May 24,

2004. www.frontpagemag.com.

102. Quoted in Stephen Holmes, "America's Blankness," *Salon*, June 17, 2004. www.salon.com.

103. Gordon Cucullu, "The Torture of Iraqi Prisoners Was an Aberration," *Front PageMagazine.com*, May 20, 2004. www.frontpagemag.com.

104. Quoted in *BBC News*, "Abu Ghraib Report: Your Reaction," August 28, 2004. http://news.bbc.co.uk.

105. Danner, "The Logic of Torture."

For Further Reading

Books

Debra Miller, *The War Against Iraq*. San Diego: Lucent, 2004. A thorough look at the buildup and events of the war.

Stacy Taus-Bolstad, *Iraq in Pictures*. Minneapolis: Lerner, 2004. A good introduction to modern-day Iraq with maps, charts, and a helpful time line.

Michael Uschan, *Life of an American Soldier in Iraq*. San Diego: Lucent, 2005. Although contributions of U.S. Air Force and Navy personnel are included, the sections on the ground troops best illustrate the difficult and dangerous job facing soldiers.

Web Sites

Amnesty International (www.amnesty.org). Monitors human rights abuses by governments around the world.

Human Rights Watch (www.hrw.org). An independent organization dedicated to investigating and exposing human rights violation worldwide.

Iraq Foundation (www.iraq foundation.org). A nonprofit, nongovernmental organization working for democracy and human rights in Iraq.

Nonviolence Web, Iraq Crisis Antiwar Homepage (www.nonviolence.org). Home to dozens of major U.S. peace groups, with articles and information about postwar Iraq.

U.S. Central Intelligence Agency (CIA) (www.cia.gov/cia/publications/factbook). A government Web site providing geographical, political, economic, and other information about Iraq.

U.S. Department of State, International Information Programs (http://usinfo.state.gov/regional/nea/iraq). A government Web site providing information about current political issues and human rights involving Iraq.

Works Consulted

Books

T.D. Allman, *Rogue State: America at War with the World*, New York: Nation, 2004. Includes a highly critical account of how the U.S. came to invade and occupy Iraq. The book does a good job of showing why so many Iraqis became disillusioned with the state of affairs after Saddam was deposed.

Wesley K. Clark, *Winning Modern Wars: Iraq, Terrorism, and the American Empire.* New York: PublicAffairs, 2003. The author, a four-star general, believes that poor postwar planning in Iraq turned many Iraqis against America and detracted from the war on terror.

Ronald D. Crelinsten and Alex P. Schmid, eds., *The Politics of Pain: Torturers and Their Masters.* San Francisco: Westview, 1995. An analysis of the rationales governments have used in the past to justify the use of torture.

Matthew McAllester, *Blinded by the Sunlight.* New York: HarperCollins, 2004. McAllester is a journalist who was imprisoned at Abu Ghraib just before the invasion of Iraq. Provides a good description of the prison during Saddam's rule and the utter helplessness and fear felt by those held there.

John Newhouse, *Imperial America: The Bush Assault on the World Order.* New York: Knopf, 2003. The author, a former foreign policy official, argues that the Bush administration's actions in Iraq have hurt the prospects for productive diplomacy in the Middle East.

Periodicals

Mike Allen and Susan Schmidt, "Memo on Interrogation Tactics Is Disavowed," *Washington Post,* June 23, 2004.

Associated Press, "Officers Directed Abu Ghraib Abuse, Witness Says," August 7, 2004.

John Barry, Mark Hosenball, and Babak Dehghanpisheh, "Abu Ghraib and Beyond," *Newsweek,* May 17, 2004.

John Barry, Michael Hirsh, and Michael Isikoff, "The Roots of Torture," *Newsweek,* May 24, 2004.

Mike Billips, "Confronting a Scandal's Debris," *Time,* May 24, 2004, p. 50.

Gordon Bishop, "America Owes No Apologies for Fighting Terrorists," *American Daily,* May 21, 2004.

Joan Biskupic, "High Court Protected Liberties by Limiting Presidential Power," *USA Today,* July 2, 2004.

Nicholas Blanford, "Iraqi Artists Depict Anger over Abu Ghraib," *Christian Science Monitor,* June 15, 2004. www.csmonitor.com.

———, "To Arabs, Photos Confirm Brutal U.S.," *Christian Science Monitor,* May 3, 2004. www.csmonitor.com.

Jess Bravin, "Pentagon Reports Set Framework for Use of Torture," *Wall Street Journal,* June 7, 2004.

Reed Brody, "Where's the Promised Accountability for U.S. Abuse of Prisoners in Iraq?" *St. Paul Pioneer Press,* August 5, 2004.

———, "Prisoners Who Disappear," *International Herald Tribune,* October 12, 2004. www.iht.com.

Mark Danner, "The Logic of Torture," *New York Review of Books,* June 24, 2004.

———, "Torture and Truth," *New York Review of Books,* June 10, 2004.

Osha Gray Davidson, "The Secret File of Abu Ghraib," *Rolling Stone,* July 28, 2004.

John Diamond, "Rumsfeld OK'd Harsh Treatment," *USA Today,* June 23, 2004. www.usatoday.com.

Mitch Frank, "A Pattern of Abuse," *Time,* May 17, 2004.

Frida Ghitis, "People Who Live in Glass Houses," *St. Louis Post-Dispatch,* May 10, 2004.

Bradley Graham, "A Failure in Leadership, All the Way Up the Ranks," *Washington Post,* August 26, 2004.

Andrew A. Green, "Md. Reservist Alerted Officers to Abuse by His Unit," *Baltimore Sun,* May 3, 2004. www. baltimoresun.com.

Thomas C. Greene, "Abu Ghraib: US Security Fiasco," *The Register,* May 24, 2004. www.theregister.co.uk.

Luke Harding, "Torture Commonplace, Say Inmates' Families," *Guardian,* May 3, 2004. www.guardian.co.uk.

Seymour Hersh, "Chain of Command," *New Yorker,* May 17, 2004. www. newyorker.com.

———, "The Gray Zone," *New Yorker,* May 24, 2004. www.newyorker.com.

———, "Torture at Abu Ghraib," *New Yorker,* May 10, 2004. www.newyorker. com.

Scott Higham and Joe Stephens, "New Details of Prison Abuse Emerge," *Washington Post,* May 21, 2004.

James Hirsch, "America Has Lost Its Moral Authority on POWs," *Boston Globe,* May 22, 2004. www.commondreams. org.

Michael Hirsh, "Grim Numbers," *Newsweek,* June 16, 2004.

Michael Hirsh and John Barry, "A Battle over Blame," *Newsweek,* August 9, 2004.

———, "The Abu Ghraib Scandal Cover-Up?" *Newsweek,* June 7, 2004.

Elizabeth Holtzman, "Bush Has a Lot to Answer for on Iraq Torture," *Newsday,* June 16, 2004.

Douglas Jehl and Kate Zernike, "Scant Evidence Cited in Long Detention of Iraqis," *New York Times,* May 30, 2004.

Charles Lane, "Justices Back Detainee Access to US Courts," *Washington Post,* June 29, 2004.

Neil A. Lewis and Eric Schmitt, "Lawyers Decided Bans on Torture Didn't Bind Bush," *New York Times,* June 8, 2004.

Adam Liptak, "Report Is Likely to Prompt Criminal Charges," *New York Times,* August 27, 2004. www.nytimes.com.

Toni Locy, "Interrogators Hid Identities," *USA Today,* May 27, 2004. www. usatoday.com.

Johanna McGeary, "The Scandal's Growing Stain," *Time*, May 17, 2004.

Greg Mitchell, "Exclusive: Shocking Details on Abuse of Reuters Staffers in Iraq," *Editor and Publisher*, May 19, 2004.

Blake Morrison and John Diamond, "Pressure at Iraqi Prison Detailed," *USA Today*, June 18, 2004. www.usatoday. com.

New York Times, "The Roots of Abu Ghraib," June 9, 2004. www.nytimes. com

Eyal Press, "In Torture We Trust," *Nation*, March 31, 2003.

Dana Priest and Barton Gellman, "US Decries Abuse but Defends Interrogations," *Washington Post*, December 26, 2002.

Dana Priest and R. Jeffrey Smith, "Memo Offered Justification for Use of Torture," *Washington Post*, June 8, 2004.

Tom Regan, "'Six Morons Who Lost the War,'" *Christian Science Monitor*, May 4, 2004. www.csmonitor.com.

Thomas E. Ricks, "Incidents Grew in Severity, Report Says," *Washington Post*, August 26, 2004.

Eric Roston and J.F.O. McAllister, "Humiliation in an Iraqi Jail," *Time*, May 10, 2004.

Rick Scavetta, "GI Flagged for Public Comment About His Abu Ghraib Experiences," *Stars and Stripes*, May 28, 2004. www.estripes.com.

R. Jeffrey Smith, "Agency Is Faulted on Practices in Iraq, Secrecy amid Probe," *Washington Post*, June 24, 2004.

———, "General Is Said to Have Urged Use of Dogs," *Washington Post*, May 26, 2004.

———, "Lawyer for State Dept. Disputed Detainee Memo," *Washington Post*, June 24, 2004.

———, "Slim Legal Grounds for Torture Memos," *Washington Post*, July 4, 2004.

St. Louis Post-Dispatch, "Prison Abuse: Passing the Buck," August 8, 2004. www.stltoday.com.

Evan Thomas, "No Good Defense," *Newsweek*, May 17, 2004.

Mark Thompson and Elaine Shannon, "The Verdict on Rumsfeld," *Time*, September 6, 2004.

Time (Canada), "Letters to the Editor," June 7, 2004.

USA Today, "How Innocent Iraqis Came to Be Abused as Terrorists," June 10, 2004.

Washington Post, "The Homicide Cases," May 28, 2004.

———, "An Inadequate Response," May 8, 2004.

———, "Key Findings," August 26, 2004.

Josh White, "Abuse Report Widens Scope of Culpability," *Washington Post*, August 26, 2004.

Josh White and Scott Higham, "Use of Dogs to Scare Prisoners Was Authorized," *Washington Post*, June 11, 2004. www.washingtonpost.com.

Josh White and Thomas E. Ricks, "Abu Ghraib Probe Points to Top Brass," *Washington Post*, August 20, 2004.

Scott Wilson, "Angry Ex-Detainees Tell of Abuse," *Washington Post*, May 3, 2004

Mortimer B. Zuckerman, "A Bit of Perspective, Please," *U.S. News & World Report*, May 24, 2004.

Internet Sources

ABCNews.com, "Lawmakers Troubled by 'Ghost Detainees,'" September 10, 2004. http://abcnews.go.com.

Al-Ahram Weekly On-Line, "MPs Slam Abu Ghraib Scandal," May 13–19, 2004. http://weekly.ahram.org.

Hannah Allam, "Dozens of Missing Iraqis Believed to Be Lost in Abu Ghraib Prison," Knight Ridder Newspapers, June 10, 2004. www.realcities.com.

BBC News, "Abu Ghraib Report: Your Reaction," August 28, 2004. http://news.bbc.co.uk.

———, "Abu Ghraib: Your Reaction." http://newsvote.bbc.co.uk.

Beliefnet, "This Is What War Looks Like." www.beliefnet.com.

Alan Bock, "Thugs with Lawyers," June 11, 2004. www.antiwar.com.

Tammy Bruce, "Why Abu Ghraib Matters," *FrontPageMagazine.com,* May 24, 2004. www.frontpagemag.com.

George W. Bush, interview by Al Arabiya Television, White House, March 12, 2004. www.whitehouse.gov.

———, remarks on efforts to globally promote women's human rights, White House, March 12, 2004. www.whitehouse.gov.

George W. Bush, remarks on Iraq at Cincinnati Museum Center, Cincinnati, Ohio, October 7, 2002. www.whitehouse.gov

Alessandro Camon, "American Torture, American Porn," *Salon,* June 7, 2004. www.salon.com.

Phillip Carter, "Cooking Up Excuses with the Pentagon," *Slate,* June 11, 2004. http://slate.msn.com.

CBSNEWS.com, "Abuse of Iraqi POWs by GIs Probed," April 28, 2004. www.cbsnews.com.

———, "GOP Sen.: 'Outraged at Outrage,'" May 11, 2004. www.cbsnews.com.

———, "Rush: MPs Just Blowing Off Steam," May 14, 2004. www.cbsnews.com.

CNN.com, "Army Report Documents Mistreatment of Iraqi Prisoners," May 4, 2004. http://edition.cnn.com.

———, "Soldier Sentenced to 1 Year in Iraqi Prisoner Abuse." www.cnn.com.

Robert Collier, "Iraqi Detainees Report 'Inhumane Treatment,'" *San Francisco Chronicle, SFGate.com,* July 29, 2003. www.sfgate.com.

Gordon Cucullu, "The Torture of Iraqi Prisoners Was an Abberation," *FrontPageMagazine.com,* May 20, 2004. www.frontpagemag.com.

Mike Ferner, "On Their Way to Abu Ghraib," *Counterpunch,* May 29–31, 2004. www.counterpunch.org.

Andrew A. Green, "Md. Reservist Alerted Officers to Alleged Abuses by His Unit," *Baltimore Sun,* May 3, 2004.

Guardian Unlimited, "Abu Ghraib General Says She's a Scapegoat," June 15, 2004. www.guardian.co.uk.

Seymour Hersh, interview with John Weisman, *Military.com,* June 1, 2004. www.military.com.

Stephen Holmes, "America's Blankness," *Salon,* June 17, 2004. www.salon.com.

House Armed Services Committee, "Statement of House Armed Services Committee Chairman Regarding Secretary of Defense Donald Rumsfeld," press release, May 7, 2004. www.whitehouse.gov.

Human Rights Watch, "The Road to Abu Ghraib." www.hrw.org.

Dahr Jamail, "The Student Is Gone; the Master Has Arrived," *NewStandard*, June 13, 2004. http//blog.newstandard news.net.

Douglas Jehl and Neil A. Lewis, "Army: Some Iraqis Exempt from Geneva," *San Diego Union-Tribune, New York Times* News Service, May 23, 2004. www. signonsandiego.com.

———, "Conventions Don't Apply to All, Red Cross Told," *San Diego Union-Tribune, New York Times* News Service, May 23, 2004. www.signonsandiego.com.

Janis Karpinski, interview on *American Morning*, transcript, CNN, May 4, 2004. http://transcripts.cnn.com.

Tom Malinowski, "Torture Guidelines," live online discussion, June 14, 2004. www.washingtonpost.com.

Andrew Marshall, "Reuters, NBC Staff Abused by US Troops in Iraq," Reuters, May 18, 2004. http://globalsecurity.com.

Nat Parry, "Bush's Apex of Unlimited Power," *Consortium News*, June 15, 2004. www.consortiumnews.com.

PBS, "Prisoner Abuse Fallout," transcript, *Online News Hour*, May 4, 2004. www.pbs.org.

Andy Rooney, "Our Darkest Days Are Here," *CBSNEWS.com*, May 23, 2004. www.cbsnews.com.

William Saletan, "Rape Rooms: A Chronology," *Slate*, May 5, 2004. http://slate.msn.com.

Josh Solomon, "US Poll of Iraqis Finds Widespread Anger at Prison Abuse, Worry About Safety," Associated Press, June 15, 2004. www.boston.com.

StarNewsOnline.com, "Unit Says It Gave Earlier Warning of Abuse," June 17, 2004. www.wilmingtonstar.com.

St. Petersburg Times Online, "The Torture Memos," June 13, 2004. www.sptimes.com.

WashingtonPost.com, "Sworn Statements by Abu Ghraib Detainees." www. washingtonpost.com.

Marian Wilkinson, "Generals in a Labyrinth of Blame," *The Age*, May 15, 2004. www.theage.com.

WorldPress.org, "Iraqi Prisoner Abuse Draws International Media Outrage," May 12, 2004. www.worldpress.org.

Index

Picture Credits

Cover photo: Getty Images
© ABC News/Charles Fredrick/Reuters/CORBIS, 55
AP/Wide World Photos, 17, 18, 22, 30, 33, 38, 54, 75, 81
Shawn Baldwin /EPA/Landov, 27
Zohra Bensemra/Reuters/Landov, 72
Courtesy of DigitalGlobe, 21 (aerial photo)
Courtesy of *Washington Post* via Getty Images, 34, 45
Larry Downing/Reuters/Landov, 49, 61, 69
Sabri Elmhedwi/EPA/Landov, 51
Chris Helgren/Reuters/Landov, 42–43
Ali Khaligh/UPI/Landov, 86
Alberto Morante/EPA/Landov, 11
Muhammed Muheisen/EPA/Landov, 23
The New Yorker/www.newyorker.com, 36, 47
Photos.com, 31 (background)
Oleg Popov/Reuters/Landov, 40
Reuters/Landov, 25, 79
Damir Sagolj/EPA/Landov, 67, 83
Getty Images, 64
Mike Theiler/EPA/Landov, 70
Roger L. Wollenberg/UPI/Landov, 58
Steve Zmina, 21, 31

About the Author

A former editor at *Reminisce* magazine, Michael J. Martin is a freelance writer whose home overlooks the Mississippi River in Lansing, Iowa. His articles have appeared in publications like *Boys' Life*, *Timeline*, and *American History*. Recent books include a history of skateboarding and another on the Emancipation Proclamation.